Teacher's Guide
Year 5 / Primary 6

Series Editor: Wendy Body

PEARSON
Longman

Carol Matchett and Gillian Howell

Starwriter at a glance

Unit	Text type	Starwriter task	Learning intention	Literacy objective
1	Reflective poem	Write a short reflective poem – rhyming or not rhyming – about the impact of a place and how it makes you feel.	To write a reflective poem that suggests thoughts or feelings.	To convey feelings, reflections or moods in a poem through the careful choice of words and phrases.
2	Metaphors	Write metaphors as complete sentences to describe a foggy day, sun over the sea, a dark windy night, a frosty winter morning.	To compose metaphors using effective images.	To write metaphors from original ideas or similes.
3	Playscript	Continue the playscript from the point where Handra is trying to calm Josie down.	To use the standard conventions of playscripts.	To write own playscript, applying conventions learned from reading; include production notes.
4	Playscript annotations	Choose a section of your playscript and add stage directions and annotations.	To annotate a playscript to help actors/readers.	To annotate a section of playscript as a preparation for performance, taking into account pace, movement, gesture and delivery of lines and the needs of the audience. To evaluate the script and the performance for their dramatic interest and impact.
5	Myth	Make a detailed plan or storyboard for the myth and write the last part of your story including an effective ending. Use a similar style to the opening of *Why Dragons Breathe Fire*.	To write the ending of the myth in the style of the opening.	To write own versions of legends, myths and fables.
6	Classic poem	Extend the poem by two or three verses at the end that explain what the person is doing in the wood, who is watching and whether or not it is an echo or someone else calling out.	To use the structure of the poem to write additional verses.	To use the structures of poems read to write extensions based on these, e.g. additional verses, or substituting own words and ideas.
7	Poem (revise and edit)	Choose a poem that you have written. Discuss with a friend anything you think could be improved. Revise and edit your poem.	To polish and improve a previously written poem.	To review and edit writing to produce a final form, matched to the needs of an identified reader.
8	Informal letter	Complete Hera's letter to her friend.	To complete a letter, in role, in an informal style.	To write from another character's point of view, e.g. retelling an incident in letter form.
9	Dialogue	Write dialogue for the extract from *Little House in the Big Woods*.	To turn reported speech into dialogue.	To write in the style of the author, e.g. writing additional dialogue.
10	Story commentary	Write a commentary on *The Little Match Girl*. Include a paragraph on the message of the story.	To write a story commentary in an impersonal style.	To write discursively about a novel or story, e.g. to describe, explain or comment on it.

Unit	Text type	Starwriter task	Learning intention	Literacy objective
11	Performance poem	Use the poem 'Fruit Picking' as a model to write one called 'Sweet Treats'.	To write a performance poem based on the structure of a model.	To use performance poems as models to write and produce poetry in polished forms through revising, redrafting and presentation.
12	Recount	Think of a match or an event you have attended recently. Write an e-mail to your best friend and a newspaper account of the same event.	To recount the same event to two different audiences, matching style to audience.	To write recounts based on subject, topic or personal experiences for (a) a close friend and (b) an unknown reader, e.g. an account of a field trip, a match, a historical event.
13	Instruction	Make sure you know how to send a text message. Write instructions for people who have their first mobile phone on how to text a friend.	To write a set of clear instructions in the correct order.	To write instructional texts, and test them out.
14	Notes	Make notes on what you have seen about the Jewish faith. Use your notes to write a report about it.	To take notes from a video clip in order to write a report.	To make notes for different purposes, e.g. noting key points as a record of what has been read, listing cues for a talk and to build on these notes in their own writing or speaking.
15	Non-chronological report	Plan and then write a report that compares the planets known as the gas giants (Jupiter, Saturn, Uranus and Neptune).	To write a non-chronological report using the standard features of reports.	To plan, compose, edit and refine short non-chronological reports.
16	Explanation	Write an introductory paragraph about wind instruments and a second paragraph to explain how they work.	To write an explanation that uses standard features including connectives to signal cause and effect.	To plan, compose, edit and refine explanatory texts.
17	Explanation (revise and edit)	Choose an explanation that you have written. Discuss with a friend anything you think could be improved. Work alone to revise and edit your explanation.	To improve clarity and check essential features of an explanation text.	To plan, compose, edit and refine explanatory texts. To evaluate their work.
18	Formal letter	Write a draft reply to support or argue an opposing point of view. Share with a friend to revise and edit before doing a final version.	To use correctly the conventions of formal letter writing.	To draft and write individual, group or class letters for real purposes, e.g. to put a point of view, comment on an emotive issue, protest; to edit and present to finished state.
19	Non-fiction commentary	Make notes as you watch the film again. Use your notes to write a commentary.	To write an objective commentary on the issues raised.	To write a commentary on an issue on paper or screen, setting out and justifying a personal view; to use structures from reading to set out and link points, e.g. numbered lists, bullet points.
20	Argument	Make notes in order to write a persuasive argument for or against: 'Should we all have the right to have fireworks?'	To write an effective argument using the standard features of a persuasive text.	To construct an argument in note form or full text to persuade others of a point of view and present the case to the class or a group; evaluate its effectiveness.

Introducing Starwriter

- ☆ Starwriter combines exciting and innovative ICT and print resources in one package to inspire and improve children's writing at KS2.

- ☆ Its major focus is helping children to create and shape texts, and deal with their structure and organisation.

- ☆ For each year group, Starwriter comprises one CD, one *Teacher's Guide* and one *Writer's Guide* for pupils. These are organised into 20 units (18 at Year 6 / Primary 7) to cover the major text types and writing composition objectives.

- ☆ Starwriter offers a simple solution to embedding both Assessment for Learning and ICT into the teaching of writing.

The underlying principles

- **INSPIRE**
  At the heart of each Starwriter unit is the multimedia stimulus, designed to capture interest, create enthusiasm and inspire children to write.

- **IMPROVE**
  Starwriter materials – in particular the *Writer's Guide* and the samples of children's writing on the CD – create a carefully structured learning experience that helps pupils become successful independent writers.

- **SUPPORT**
  Starwriter supports teachers with innovative resources that are easy to use, and practical and straightforward guidance. In this *Teacher's Guide* there are two double-page spreads to support each unit; one on Planning and Teaching and one on Assessing and Improving.

Other key features

- ☆ Starwriter supports the transition from shared to independent writing.

- ☆ It promotes creative thinking and encourages critical reflection.

- ☆ It makes meaningful cross-curricular links. Subject matter from other curriculum areas provides stimuli for non-fiction writing and encourages pupils to draw on their knowledge of these subjects to provide content for their written texts.

- ☆ The images and audio of the fiction, poetry or non-fiction stimuli can also be used as starting points for activities or creative responses in drama, music or art.

- ☆ Starwriter embeds Assessment for Learning into the teaching and learning cycle. It helps children to understand the learning objectives and how to achieve them, with opportunities for revision and improvement built into each unit.

- ☆ It encourages speaking and listening by providing opportunities and starting points for all aspects. For example:

  - ○ preparing oral presentations to accompany the images in the stimulus
  - ○ exploring ideas through discussion
  - ○ listening, remembering and responding to the audio
  - ○ discussing use of language and music
  - ○ using role play and other drama techniques to explore ideas and situations shown on screen.

Starwriter features two appealing characters as linking devices or presenters. The male is called Cygnus (after the name of the biggest star in the universe) and the female is called Alpha (after the name of the brightest star in any constellation).

- ☆ Starwriter combines elements that appeal to all learning styles:

  - ○ **Visual:** through seeing images and texts, and watching demonstrations on screen.
  - ○ **Auditory:** through listening to audio and discussion prompted by the stimulus.
  - ○ **Kinaesthetic:** through using the tools to actively engage with the images and text.

★ Suggested route through the Starwriter materials

Introduce the task → Use the stimulus

↓

Read and discuss the *Writer's Guide* spread ← Carry out the Shared Writing activity

↓

Children write independently   → Children evaluate their writing using the 'Check it out' and 'Talk it over' sections of the *Writer's Guide*

 ↓

- Revisit the stimulus for a different purpose
- Use the Image Bank
- Revisit the Writing Sample (in small groups, for example)

 ← As a class, discuss, revise and improve the Writing Sample

---

Starwriter allows the flexibility to use alternative routes. For example, some teachers may wish to introduce or revise a text type using the 'Style guide' section of the *Writer's Guide* before the children see the stimulus. Others may choose to work with the Writing Sample before children write independently – perhaps with children needing extra support. The Planning and Teaching pages also include suggestions for additional writing tasks for each stimulus.

Using the Interactive CD-ROM

What's on it?

The Starwriter CD-ROM for Year 5 / Primary 6 contains:

- 20 multimedia stimuli – one per unit
- a Shared Writing screen to support each unit
- a child's Writing Sample for each of the 20 tasks
- an Image Bank
- a Notebook.

The stimulus

The multimedia stimulus combines the images and audio of animation or video with an on-screen text or extract. It provides a lively and motivating context for the writing task that follows.

- **visual** images create 'mental pictures' that pupils can draw on when writing. Use them as a shared focus for developing ideas for writing and creative thinking in response to the task.
- **audio** helps establish mood and voice; encourage children to hold this in their head and imitate and respond to it in their own writing.
- **text** extracts model a style and connect writing to reading; encourage analysis of what makes writing effective so that children can apply it to their own writing.

The multimedia presentations **stimulate thinking**, encourage **talk for writing** and develop **ideas for writing**. For example:

- Encourage pupils to talk about what they see and hear and how it makes them feel. What does it make them think about? Use 'think, pair and share' strategies to encourage all pupils to respond.
- Use prompts and open questions to help children think creatively around the stimulus, developing ideas to use when writing. For example, *What happened before/what happens next? Look outside the image; look/think from a different point of view.* Allow 'thinking time' to encourage thoughtful and creative responses to the prompts.
- Use the on-screen prompts and the text to focus on how children will use these ideas in their writing. Encourage pupils to try out ideas orally before writing.

The tools

The stimulus is accompanied by a bank of tools which can be used to annotate the text and images on screen. They can be used to encourage interactive whole-class teaching, for example:

- to prompt discussion and develop thinking around the on-screen images (e.g. thought and speech bubbles)
- to involve children in annotating the text or marking details in the images to help focus on particular features (e.g. the highlighter, pencil or label tools)
- to brainstorm, prompt alternative suggestions or collect possibilities (e.g. the sticky note or the hide/reveal text tool).

Read me document

For detailed guidance on using the Starwriter CD-ROM, including loading, saving, passwords and general troubleshooting, please see the Read me document on the CD itself.

Text tab

Displays the stimulus text for editing without visuals.

Volume control

Click on this button to bring up a slide volume control.

Save

Click here to save work.

Reset

Return the page to its original state with no annotations.

Audio Off/On

Allows viewing of the stimulus with sound on or off.

Screen On/Off

Select Screen Off for audio only.

Speech bubble, thought bubble, sticky note, label

Add to text or pictures, to use as prompts, type in ideas or keep notes of important points. Click to select, then click again to place the shape. You can type inside, resize, or move the shape around the screen.

Eraser

Use this tool to 'rub out' pencil marks.

Pencil

Use the different colours to annotate text or pictures.

Bin

Use this tool to delete annotations.

Note tab

Every time you add an annotation, it is automatically marked with a small, orange triangle here. A Note tab will also appear underneath the scroll bar, which you can name. Click on the Note to recall that particular screen, or scroll back and forwards through your notes using the arrows to the left.

Rewind/Fast forward

Click on these to move the material forwards and backwards. You can also click and drag the thumbtrack (red circle) in the green scroll bar for this.

Play/Pause

Click to play the stimulus. The button becomes a pause button: click to pause for discussion or to annotate.

Stimulus | Text

Unit 8 Informal Letter

Note 1

Main Menu | Unit Menu | Shared Writing | Writing Sample | Image Bank | Notebook

Shared Writing

What's on it?

Each stimulus is linked to a Shared Writing screen. This might show a planning framework, the opening to a story or a few lines of a poem.

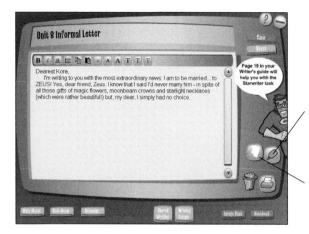

Highlighter

Use this tool to highlight key words or sections of the text.

Hide/reveal text

Use this tool to cover words or block out sentences in the text, then reveal them.

The Shared Writing screen helps to make the link from the whole-class discussion of the stimulus and Starwriter task to the children's independent writing. You can show pupils how to start shaping ideas into the written form required, focusing on text structure and organisation, language choices and/or sentence structures.

You can vary your use of the Shared Writing screen to match the needs of pupils. For example, to support those who require careful scaffolding, use shared and supported composition to add to the text on screen. Move other pupils quickly on to writing independently using the *Writer's Guide*.

The Shared Writing screen helps you to make sure all the children are clear about the task and how to go about it before they begin, building confidence and certainty.

Starwriter on KnowledgeBox

Accessing the modules

Starwriter modules are accessed through the KnowledgeBox Contents panel.
Find the module in the list.
Click on the **View** button to reveal the folders of content.

Differences in functionality

Minimise

The minimise button is not available on Starwriter resources on KnowledgeBox.

Save

KnowledgeBox only allows you to save a single version of a resource. This means that each time you decide to save a resource you will be overwriting any versions you have saved previously.

The Image Bank

Each CD contains an interactive bank of backgrounds, characters, props and sounds to allow children to plan, create and write independently. These are found in the Image Bank.

The Image Bank develops creative thinking and provides opportunities for pupils to choose their own starting points for writing.

- Images can be combined on screen enabling children to build their own pictures. Text and sounds can be added to create storyboards or a sequence of linked screens for a multimedia presentation.
- Children can use the Image Bank functionality to compose and edit complete texts on screen.
- It can be used to stimulate ideas for writing (e.g. combining elements to create new scenarios or planning a text in storyboard form that can then be worked on away from the computer).

Click on these buttons to bring up a selection of backgrounds, characters or props. Once on screen, characters and props can be moved around and/or resized as desired.

Click here to call up a list of sound effects to add to your screen. Once selected, click on the megaphone icon to activate the effect.

Add text in speech or thought bubbles, to make storyboards or comic strip stories, for example. Add labels to the screen, for non-narrative presentations for example, or as notes if using the Image Bank for planning.

Customise the selected image by flipping or rotating it.

Children add a title and their name here.

Click here to type text to accompany each picture (e.g. notes for a storyboard, text for a comic-strip story or on-screen presentation).

View the sequence of screens in presentation mode.

Create a series of up to ten screens, to tell a story or present a sequence of points in a non-narrative text.

Contents of the Image Bank

Backgrounds (10)	Props (20)	Characters (20)	Sound effects (20)
Blank	Mobile phone	Cygnus (male)	Water lapping
Woodland scene	Thunderbolts	Cygnus in different pose	Heavy rainfall
Rural scene	Magical apple tree	Alpha (female)	Horses' hooves
Empty street	Tractor	Oliver Twist	Thunderclaps/storm
Park scene	Alien spaceship	Red Riding Hood	Bird song
Classroom scene	Christmas tree and parcels	Ballet dancer	Text alert
Theatre stage	Alien planet	Girl	Mobile ring-tone
Fields	Charm bracelet	Girl on phone	Dragon roar
Planets	Door	Cuckoo	Sleigh bells
Winter landscape	Key	Farmer	Fireworks and crowd
with house	Wardrobe	Man	Ambulance siren
	Stars	Boy	Church bells
	Strawberry	Woman	Wolf roar
	Gooseberry	Robot	Spaceship
	Sweets	Wizard	Children playing
	Matches	Queen	School bell
	Scroll	Monster	Dog barking
	Coffee mug	King	Footsteps
	Panpipes	Alien	Aeroplane
	Recorder	Dragon	Door opens/closes

The Writing Sample

The Writing Sample for each unit is an example of a child's writing in response to the Starwriter task. The samples:

- are fully editable
- were written by children from a range of schools
- retain the original errors and organisation
- are presented in a typed form to make them editable on screen
- were chosen to allow room for improvement or development – they were not the best examples produced by the schools.

Ros Wilson

The Writing Samples were marked by Ros Wilson of *2020 Vision* and her colleagues, using the acclaimed Criterion Scale she developed as a formative assessment tool to improve children's writing. A thorough explanation of the scale can be found in *Strategies for Immediate Impact on Writing Standards* (Andrell Education 2002, ISBN 0954 701909).

Where possible, the samples have been levelled and targets for improvement are suggested. Click on the 'Target and Level' tab to access these comments. The targets for improvement often make reference to 'wow' words and 'power openers'. For those unfamiliar with Ros Wilson's terminology, 'wow' words are simply examples of rich vocabulary. Power openers are the use of powerful connectives, 'ly' words and 'ing' words to start sentences.

Using the sample

The samples are intended to help you teach the skills of revising and editing and, importantly, to support 'assess, revise and improve' strategies with the class:

- Show the sample in the 'Revise and Edit' screen and ask the children to comment on it in relation to the task and learning objectives. Be specific about what you want the children to comment on, such as structure and organisation or vocabulary choices.
- Adopt a 'praise first' strategy, where the children first identify something that works and then find something that can be improved or developed. For example: *Give stars for good writing when you've read it all through, then make suggestions to improve something too.* This helps establish the process as a positive and constructive activity, rather than a critical, negative one.
- Having identified what could be improved, discuss how this could be done. Encourage the children to suggest and make changes on screen to improve the text.
- In the 'Target and Level' section, share and discuss the level information and compare the suggested targets with what the children identified as areas for improvement.
- Ask the children to apply the same 'assess, revise and improve' strategies to their own work, either working independently or with partners.

The Assessing and Improving pages of this guide give practical suggestions for discussing each Writing Sample. While working on a piece of writing, you may wish to revisit a sample more than once as part of a cycle of 'review, teach, learn'. For example: to focus on a different aspect of the writing, to deepen understanding or to revise the standard features of a particular form.

Using the Writing Sample helps children to:

- learn to judge for themselves what works and what needs to be improved
- move forward in their understanding of what it is that makes a particular piece of writing successful
- adopt the 'assess, revise and improve' philosophy and apply the same strategies to their own work.

Echo

"Who's there?" I questioned,
"Who's there? Who's there?" it followed,
The breeze pushed past my feathers,
I just sat there and sorrowed.

"Answer me now!" I demanded,
"Answer me now! Answer me now! Answer me now."
I couldn't bear this mockery any more,
And with that I flew home in fear and
not knowing how.

Author

Smart thinker,
Word drinker.
Nail biter,
Pen fighter.
Quick scribbler,
Pencil nibbler.
Book Lover,
Award winner,
Determined finisher.
Deadline meeter.
writing beater.
Paper scruncher,
biscuit muncher.
Sweat ~~taker~~ maker,
trophy taker.

The *Writer's Guide* is an ongoing reference book or support manual for pupils. It gives them direct guidance and advice on tackling both the Starwriter tasks and writing generally. It includes some generic summary pages as well as the specific unit spreads.

Unit title

States the objective of the unit. An abbreviated form of the learning intention given in the *Teacher's Guide*.

Extract

Reminds children of the stimulus and shows features of the text type in action.

Style guide

Describes the standard features of the particular text type or writing form.

Starwriter task

The task is aimed at pupils of average ability; differentiated versions of the task for higher and lower achievers are given in this *Teacher's Guide*.

Helping hand

Helpful hints and pointers to support children in the task.

Check it out

Questions to help pupils check whether or not their writing is successful. Helps to support self and peer assessment.

Talk it over

Questions to help children reflect on their writing and the writing process.

Starwriter starburst

Rhyming couplet designed to encapsulate an important piece of advice in a memorable form.

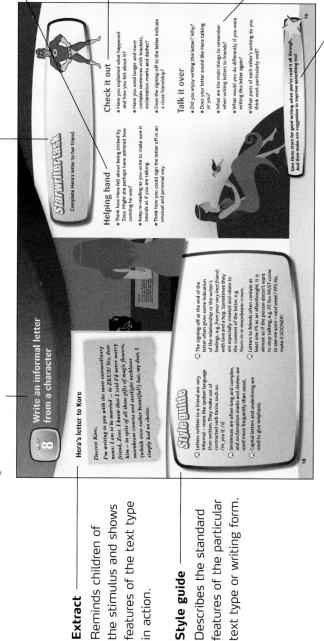

Supporting independent writing

The *Writer's Guide* supports pupils at all stages of the writing process:

Before writing	Use the 'Style guide' and text extract to help focus on the structure, organisation and language features required for that text type.
Planning and drafting	Encourage the children to refer to the *Writer's Guide* as they write. It reminds them of key points and will help them make decisions about organisation and language features as they work. Draw attention to the 'Helping hand' section which gives some task-specific points to think about.
Revising and editing	Encourage the children to see revising and editing as an ongoing process, rather than something just done at the end. Remind them to keep referring to the *Writer's Guide* to check they are on the right track and have remembered the key points. The 'Check it out' section will help them to evaluate their work and give specific points to help them improve it.
After writing	Encourage the children to reflect on a task once completed, and think about how it has contributed to their learning and/or growth as writers. The 'Talk it over' section is designed to encourage children to reflect in pairs or small groups on what they have learned, what was successful, why it worked and what they need to learn next. The practice of having an identified talk partner is strongly recommended.

When you first introduce the *Writer's Guide*, you may need to model or share this process with the children as they proceed through a writing task. As they become used to the format, children should be encouraged to use the *Writer's Guide* independently – not just when completing Starwriter tasks, but also when writing in other curriculum areas.

Once the process is established, the *Writer's Guide* promotes independence. Its use will help to:

  o teach pupils the key features to remember about various text types or writing forms, thus enabling them to use and adapt a range of forms
  o maintain their focus on the task
  o show them how to work things out for themselves
  o encourage self-evaluation, and the understanding that it is the writer who has the choice and responsibility when it comes to developing and improving his or her skills.

Starwriter and the Scottish guidelines

'Any worthwhile language activity will move in and out of outcomes and through varying combinations of strands.' (5–14 English Language Guidelines, SOED1991)

Starwriter Year 5 / Primary 6 provides stimulating writing tasks particularly suitable for pupils working towards Scottish 5–14 Level D. The tasks touch upon various strands in the other English Language outcomes of Reading, Talking and Listening. These are included in the overview chart below. The technical skills of Punctuation and Structure, Spelling and Presentation are practised throughout.

Unit	Text type	Starwriter task	5–14 Literacy Outcomes/Strands (R) Reading, (T) Talking, (L) Listening	5–14 Writing Attainment Targets
1	Reflective poem	Write a short reflective poem – rhyming or not rhyming – about the impact of a place and how it makes you feel.	(R) Reading to reflect on the writer's ideas and craft, Knowledge about language (T) Talking about texts (L) Listening in order to respond to texts	**Personal Writing (Level D)** write about personal experiences, expressing thoughts and feelings for a specific purpose and audience and using appropriate organisation and vocabulary.
2	Metaphors	Write metaphors as complete sentences to describe a foggy day, sun over the sea, a dark windy night, a frosty winter morning.	(R) Reading to reflect on the writer's ideas and craft, Knowledge about language	
3	Playscript	Continue the playscript from the point where Handra is trying to calm Josie down.	(R) Reading to reflect on the writer's ideas and craft, Awareness of genre (T) Talking about texts (L) Awareness of genre	
4	Playscript annotations	Choose a section of your playscript and add stage directions and annotations.	(R) Knowledge about language (T) Talking about texts (L) Awareness of genre	
5	Myth	Make a detailed plan or storyboard for the myth and write the last part of your story including an effective ending. Use a similar style to the opening of *Why Dragons Breathe Fire*.	(L) Awareness of genre	**Imaginative Writing (Level D)** write imaginative pieces in various genres, using appropriate organisation and vocabulary
6	Classic poem	Extend the poem by two or three verses at the end that explain what the person is doing in the wood, who is watching and whether or not it is an echo or someone else calling out.	(R) Reading to reflect on the writer's ideas and craft (T) Talking about texts (L) Listening in order to respond to texts	
7	Poem (revise and edit)	Choose a poem that you have written. Discuss with a friend anything you think could be improved. Revise and edit your poem.	(R) Reading to reflect on the writer's ideas and craft (T) Talking about texts (L) Listening in order to respond to texts	
8	Informal letter	Complete Hera's letter to her friend.	(R) Reading to reflect on the writer's ideas and craft, Knowledge about language (T) Talking about texts	
9	Dialogue	Write dialogue for the extract from *Little House in the Big Woods*.	(R) Reading to reflect on the writer's ideas and craft (T) Talking about texts	

Unit	Text type	Starwriter task	5–14 Literacy Outcomes/Strands (R) Reading, (T) Talking, (L) Listening	5–14 Writing Attainment Targets
10	Story commentary	Write a commentary on *The Little Match Girl*. Include a paragraph on the message of the story.	(R) Reading to reflect on the writer's ideas and craft (T) Talking about texts (L) Listening in order to respond to texts	**Functional Writing (Level D)** write in a variety of forms to communicate key events, facts or ideas, using appropriate organisation and vocabulary.
11	Performance poem	Use the poem *'Fruit Picking'* as a model to write one called *'Sweet Treats'*.	(R) Awareness of genre (T) Audience awareness (L) Listening in order to respond to texts	**Imaginative Writing (Level D)** write imaginative pieces in various genres, using appropriate organisation and vocabulary
12	Recount	Think of a match or an event you have attended recently. Write an e-mail to your best friend and a newspaper account of the same event.	(R) Awareness of genre	
13	Instruction	Make sure you know how to send a text message. Write instructions for people who have their first mobile phone on how to text a friend.	(R) Awareness of genre (T) Conveying information, instructions and directions (L) Listening for information, instructions and directions	
14	Notes	Make notes on what you have seen about the Jewish faith. Use your notes to write a report about it.	(L) Listening for information, instructions and directions	
15	Non-chronological report	Plan and then write a report that compares the planets known as the gas giants (Jupiter, Saturn, Uranus and Neptune).	(L) Listening for information, instructions and directions	
16	Explanation	Write an introductory paragraph about wind instruments and a second paragraph to explain how they work.	(R) Awareness of genre (T) Conveying information, instructions and directions	**Functional Writing (Level D)** write in a variety of forms to communicate key events, facts or ideas, using appropriate organisation and vocabulary.
17	Explanation (revise and edit)	Choose an explanation that you have written. Discuss with a friend anything you think could be improved. Work alone to revise and edit your explanation.	(R) Reading to reflect on the writer's ideas and craft	
18	Formal letter	Write a draft reply to support or argue an opposing point of view. Share with a friend to revise and edit before doing a final version.	(R) Knowledge about language	
19	Non-fiction commentary	Make notes as you watch the film again. Use your notes to write a commentary.	(L) Listening in order to respond to texts	
20	Argument	Make notes in order to write a persuasive argument for or against: 'Should we all have the right to have fireworks?'	(T) Talking in groups (L) Listening in groups	

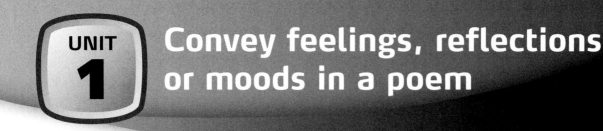

Convey feelings, reflections or moods in a poem

Planning and Teaching

Text type	Reflective poem
Literacy objective	To convey feelings, reflections or moods in a poem through the careful choice of words and phrases.
Starwriter task	Write a short reflective poem – rhyming or not rhyming – about the impact of a place and how it makes you feel.
Suggestions for differentiation	▲ Write a reflective poem with the same rhyming scheme or pattern as 'Symphony in Yellow' about the impact of a place and how it makes you feel. ▼ List some interesting words, phrases or sentences that describe a place you know well and how it makes you feel. Use your list to write a poem.

Using the CD

Stimulus description

- An illustrated reading of 'Symphony in Yellow' by Oscar Wilde is shown.
- Text of the poem appears on screen.
- Images appear on screen to encourage the children to think about a place that inspires them.

Using the Starwriter stimulus

- Select 'Screen Off' and play audio only. Ask the children to visualise the scene being described. *What images does it bring to mind? What mood is created? How is it created?*
- Return to the start of the poem. Select 'Screen On' to play the video as well as audio. Discuss how the images fit the text and vice versa.
- Ask the children to underline or circle phrases that convey mood or feelings using the pencil tool and explain their choices.
- Encourage the children to 'think, pair and share' ideas. *How do you know this is a poem? Why has the poet written this poem? What does the poet think or feel about this place?*
- Choose one of the photos from the end of the video to discuss. *What does this place make you think about? What mood or atmosphere would you associate it with?* Use thought bubbles to record the children's thoughts. Use sticky notes to add 'mood words' and descriptive phrases to the photo.
- Show any of the images and ask the children to imagine stepping into the scene and turning around. *What do you see, hear, feel, smell?* Ask them to record words on their individual whiteboards. Get them to focus on interesting details in the image and record words or phrases on their whiteboards to describe them.

Using Shared Writing

The Shared Writing section includes an image of a quiet city very early in the morning.

- Refer to the first verse to remind the children of the reflective quality of the poem.
- Add bullet-pointed notes describing what can be seen, heard, felt and smelled.
- Insert adjectives and adjectival phrases, encouraging the children to use similes and metaphors in the description.

Revisiting and extending the stimulus

- Imagine that instead of a poem this was the setting for the first part of a story. Write an opening paragraph describing the setting.
- Imagine the photos are part of a travel brochure. Write the accompanying text to persuade people to visit these places.
- Write the dialogue for a phone conversation in which one person tells another about a recent visit or day out.

Writer's Guide: Support for the Task

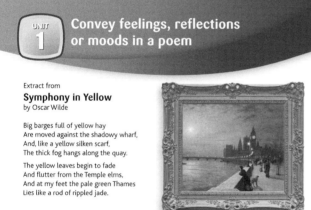

UNIT 1

Convey feelings, reflections or moods in a poem

Starwriter task

Write a short reflective poem – rhyming or not rhyming – about the impact of a place and how it makes you feel.

Extract from
Symphony in Yellow
by Oscar Wilde

Big barges full of yellow hay
Are moved against the shadowy wharf,
And, like a yellow silken scarf,
The thick fog hangs along the quay.

The yellow leaves begin to fade
And flutter from the Temple elms,
And at my feet the pale green Thames
Lies like a rod of rippled jade.

Helping hand

- Visualise your subject in detail. Jot down the things that have an immediate effect and how the place makes you feel. Does it bring back any particular memories?
- What colours, shapes or movements can you see?
- How could you describe what you see/hear/smell/touch? Does it remind you of anything else? Could you use a simile or metaphor?

Check it out

- Have you chosen the best, most unusual, and most interesting combinations of words?
- Have you used any similes or metaphors? Have you used too many similes or metaphors?!
- Could someone else tell how you feel about this place from reading your poem?

Talk it over

- Discuss the mood or atmosphere in the poem. Is it what you intended?
- Which is the most successful part of your poem and why?
- What aspect of this piece of writing did you find the most difficult?
- Has talking about it made you want to change anything in the poem?

Style guide

- *Reflect* means *think* or *consider*, so a reflective poem makes you look at something or someone in a different way by sharing the poet's views, thoughts, feelings and images.
- Reflective poems have a particular mood or atmosphere, e.g. calm, peaceful, tranquil, sad, regretful, inspirational.
- Similes and metaphors are often used to convey an idea, to invite a new or unusual way of looking at something or to create a memorable image.
- The sounds of words can suggest a mood. For example, words with long vowel sounds help to suggest peaceful or calm moods: *the pale green Thames lies* ... Words with short vowel sounds can create the opposite effect: *little restless midges*.
- Reflective poetry can take different forms and structures. Oscar Wilde's poem has three stanzas with a rhyming scheme or pattern of ABBA.

Reading your writing aloud in your head
Helps you find any problems with what you have said.

4   5

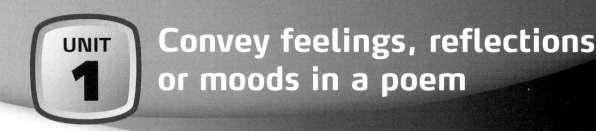

Assessing and Improving

Starwriter task	Write a short reflective poem – rhyming or not rhyming – about the impact of a place and how it makes you feel.
Learning intention	To write a reflective poem that suggests thoughts or feelings.
Success criteria *Writer's Guide: 'Check it Out'*	• Have you chosen the best, most unusual and most interesting combination of words? • Have you used any similes or metaphors? Have you used too many similes or metaphors? • Could someone else tell how you feel about this place from reading your poem?
Review with talk partner *Writer's Guide: 'Talk it Over'*	• Discuss the mood or atmosphere in the poem. Is it what you intended? • Which is the most successful part of your poem and why? • What aspect of this piece of writing did you find the most difficult? • Has talking about it made you want to change anything in the poem? What and why?

? Children's Understanding of the Text Type

Main features

- Poems have a form and structure, but there are many different forms and structures to choose from.
- Words are chosen for the sound patterns they make as well as their meaning (e.g. rhyme, rhythm, alliteration).
- Some poems follow a strict rhyme scheme, but not all poems have to rhyme.

How is poetry different from prose?

- A prose description is written in running sentences; a poem is written in lines.
- A prose description links together all the words, phrases and sentences; in a poem, a phrase can be a line by itself.

What is special about a reflective poem?

- Reflective poems have a particular mood or atmosphere.
- In a reflective poem the reader shares the poet's views, thoughts, feelings and images about the place or person being described.
- Words are chosen for the feeling and mood they suggest as well as their meaning.

Learning from the Writing Sample on the CD

Discuss and revise

- Read the poem aloud. *What mood or feelings does it convey? Does the mood come across strongly or could it be improved or strengthened? How?* For example:
  - add words to suggest the mood rather than just describing what the place is like
  - add words with sound qualities, e.g. soft, soothing 's' sounds or wild, windy 'w' words; slow calm, long vowel sounds or quick, rapid short vowel sounds.

Grammar, spelling, punctuation and layout

- Ask the children to identify examples of interesting words and explain why they work. *Which words or phrases could be improved? How?* For example:
  - use personification, metaphor or similes (to describe the river, or the insects, for example)
  - add expressive adjectives
  - replace weak verbs with powerful ones
  - move words around to make interesting combinations
  - add words linked to different senses
  - add words chosen for their sound as well as their meaning
  - delete anything that doesn't work – make every word count.
- *Are all the words spelled correctly?*
- Ask the children to focus on the punctuation. *Are commas used correctly? What other sorts of punctuation could be used to improve the poem?*

Key Vocabulary

reflective	form	simile
image	structure	metaphor
mood	rhyme	atmosphere
stanza	alliteration	cliché

Write metaphors

Planning and Teaching

Text type	Metaphors
Literacy objective	To write metaphors from original ideas or similes.
Starwriter task	Write metaphors as complete sentences to describe a foggy day, sun over the sea, a dark windy night, a frosty winter morning.
Suggestions for differentiation	▲ Write metaphors about a storm to make into a short poem. ▼ Write metaphors about: thunder as if it were a giant, snow as if it were cotton wool, frost as if it were sugar, rain as if it were tears.

Using the CD

Stimulus description

- Descriptive metaphors are read over animated weather scenes.
- The text of each metaphor appears on screen.
- Weather words appear on screen to inspire the children to write their own metaphors.

Using the Starwriter stimulus

- Show the five weather animations without audio. Encourage the children to 'think, pair and share' their impressions of each scene. *What do you notice first? How does this image make you feel?*
- Return to the start of the video and play it with audio. *Which metaphor sticks in your mind? Why?*
- Show the text of each metaphor. Discuss why it was chosen. *What do metaphors describe? Sights, sounds, feelings, moods or a combination of things?*
- Click on the text tab. Ask the children to highlight powerful verbs in one colour and adjectival phrases in a different colour (hold down the pencil button to select other colours).
- Choose one animation to show again. Encourage the children to 'step into' the picture and look around, using all their senses. *Look for another detail to describe using a simile or metaphor.* Record the children's ideas in thought bubbles around the image.
- Show the word sequence at the end of the stimulus. Ask the children to create in their mind a video sequence for one of these images. *Fade up your image ... pan across your image ... zoom out ... turn up the sound effects. What do you notice, hear, feel?*
- Encourage the children to suggest ideas for similes (e.g. 'Hail is like ... because ... '). Record suggestions on labels attached to each word. Discuss how to develop these similes into longer metaphors.
- Discuss how each word is animated to suggest the type of weather. *If it were a person what sort of person would it be? How would it behave?* Use sticky notes to record ideas for personification.

Using Shared Writing

The Shared Writing section re-uses the final metaphor as an example to encourage the children to write their own metaphors.

- Select a noun from the list to be used in a metaphor for a frosty morning.
- Highlight 'fog', 'sun' and 'wind'. List adjectives that could be used to make descriptive noun phrases.
- Ask the children to compare the noun phrases. Take suggestions of verbs to use when writing the comparisons as metaphors.

Revisiting and extending the stimulus

- Write a haiku poem to accompany each weather scene. Read the poems over the images or type them on sticky notes attached to the image.
- Choose one of the images from the video to use as the starting point for a story.
- Select one of the images to use for a news report about the weather. Write the accompanying voiceover or script, giving details about the problems caused by the day's weather.
- Imagine that rather than writing descriptively about the weather, you are writing a factual report on weather. Write the text to accompany the images, giving factual information about different types of weather.

📖 Writer's Guide: Support for the Task

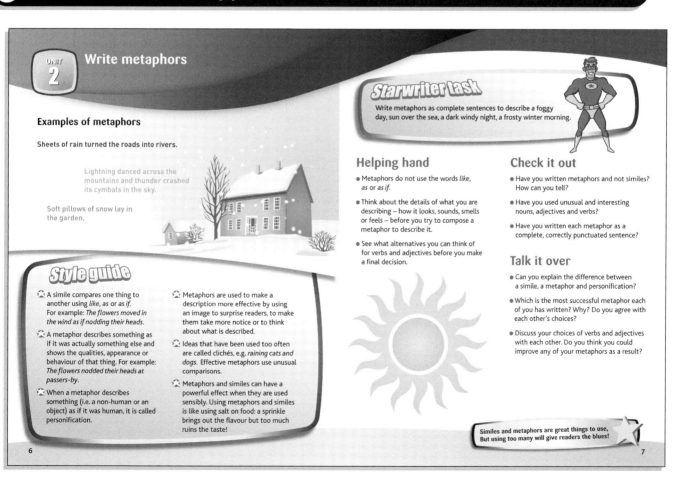

UNIT 2 **Write metaphors**

Examples of metaphors

Sheets of rain turned the roads into rivers.

Lightning danced across the mountains and thunder crashed its cymbals in the sky.

Soft pillows of snow lay in the garden.

Style guide

- A simile compares one thing to another using *like*, *as* or *as if*. For example: *The flowers moved in the wind as if nodding their heads.*
- A metaphor describes something as if it was actually something else and shows the qualities, appearance or behaviour of that thing. For example: *The flowers nodded their heads at passers-by.*
- When a metaphor describes something (i.e. a non-human or an object) as if it was human, it is called personification.

- Metaphors are used to make a description more effective by using an image to surprise readers, to make them take more notice or to think about what is described.
- Ideas that have been used too often are called clichés, e.g. *raining cats and dogs*. Effective metaphors use unusual comparisons.
- Metaphors and similes can have a powerful effect when they are used sensibly. Using metaphors and similes is like using salt on food: a sprinkle brings out the flavour but too much ruins the taste!

Starwriter task

Write metaphors as complete sentences to describe a foggy day, sun over the sea, a dark windy night, a frosty winter morning.

Helping hand

- Metaphors do not use the words *like*, *as* or *as if*.
- Think about the details of what you are describing – how it looks, sounds, smells or feels – before you try to compose a metaphor to describe it.
- See what alternatives you can think of for verbs and adjectives before you make a final decision.

Check it out

- Have you written metaphors and not similes? How can you tell?
- Have you used unusual and interesting nouns, adjectives and verbs?
- Have you written each metaphor as a complete, correctly punctuated sentence?

Talk it over

- Can you explain the difference between a simile, a metaphor and personification?
- Which is the most successful metaphor each of you has written? Why? Do you agree with each other's choices?
- Discuss your choices of verbs and adjectives with each other. Do you think you could improve any of your metaphors as a result?

Similes and metaphors are great things to use, But using too many will give readers the blues!

6

7

Write metaphors

Assessing and Improving

Starwriter task	Write metaphors as complete sentences to describe a foggy day, sun over the sea, a dark windy night, a frosty winter morning.
Learning intention	To compose metaphors using effective images.
Success criteria *Writer's Guide: 'Check it Out'*	• Have you written metaphors and not similes? How can you tell? • Have you used unusual and interesting nouns, adjectives and verbs? • Have you written each metaphor as a complete, correctly punctuated sentence?
Review with talk partner *Writer's Guide: 'Talk it Over'*	• Can you explain the difference between a simile, a metaphor and personification? • Which is the most successful metaphor each of you has written? Why? Do you agree with each other's choices? • Discuss your choices of verbs and adjectives with each other. Do you think you could improve any of your metaphors as a result?

? Children's Understanding of the Text Type

Main features

- Metaphors are a descriptive device that 'show' an image rather than 'tell about' the image.

- They can surprise the reader and make them think twice.

- They can enhance poetry writing or narrative prose.

- They convey an image using few words.

How do metaphors and similes differ?

- A simile is an explicit description where one thing is compared to another, using 'like', 'as' or 'as if'.

- A metaphor implies that one thing is actually something else by giving it the appearance, characteristics or behaviour of something else.

Learning from the Writing Sample on the CD

Discuss and revise

- Read the metaphor aloud. *Why is this a metaphor rather than a simile? What image does it create? Does the image work? How could it be improved?* For example:
  - ○ replace any common or clichéd metaphors with something more unusual, creative or surprising
  - ○ use personification
  - ○ develop an idea or extend a simple metaphor.

Grammar, spelling, punctuation and layout

- Ask the children to identify which words are good examples and explain why. *Which words could be improved? How?* For example:
  - ○ replace weak verbs with more powerful ones
  - ○ use adverbs to enhance verbs
  - ○ choose adjectives to enhance nouns
  - ○ experiment with different adjectives or more precise nouns.
- *Do the metaphor words create a 'mood'?*
- Change adjectives and adverbial phrases to affect the mood.
- Experiment with deleting unnecessary words.

Key Vocabulary

metaphor	image
simile	comparison
cliché	mood
personification	

Write a playscript

Planning and Teaching

Text type	Playscript
Literacy objective	To write own playscript, applying conventions learned from reading; include production notes.
Starwriter task	Continue the playscript from the point where Handra is trying to calm Josie down.
Suggestions for differentiation	▲ Write the playscript for *Invitation to Tea* based on the outline you have seen. ▼ In your own words, write the first part of the play where Josie is telling Handra how cross she is about the boys not turning up.

Using the CD

Stimulus description

- An audio reading of the story *Invitation to Tea* accompanies a sequence of images.
- The opening to a playscript based on the story appears on screen.

Using the Starwriter stimulus

- Play the stimulus. Ask the children to compare the start of the script and the start of the story. *How are they different in terms of dialogue, narration and introduction of setting?*

- Show the text of the script. Use the highlighter and pencil tools to annotate the key features of playscripts (e.g. scene number, scene setting, layout of dialogue).

- Ask the children to read the script with a partner, using appropriate expression. *The story told us 'Josie is very angry'. How can we tell this from what she says in the script?*

- Return to the start and play the first part of the story again where the girls are in the playground. *What are the two characters thinking/feeling at this point?* Encourage the children to freeze-frame the scene and thought-track the characters. Use thought bubbles to record ideas on screen.

- Show a picture of the girls in the playground. Discuss how thoughts, feelings and events can be conveyed through dialogue. *The story tells us that 'Handra tries to calm Josie down'. What might Handra say? How will Josie respond?* Encourage the children to develop ideas through role play. Use speech bubbles to record ideas on screen. Use contracted forms to make the dialogue sound natural.

- Continue to show the sequence of images. Encourage the children to pick out the main points they need to convey in their playscript. Attach a sticky note to each picture and note down key points.

- Show picture three (after Josie has received the text message). Attach a thought and speech bubble to the picture. *What is Josie thinking now? How can we show this through what she says?*

Using Shared Writing

The Shared Writing section provides the beginning of the playscript as a model for continuing the script.

- Highlight the names of the characters. Ask the children who will be speaking next, where to write the name and how to differentiate it from the dialogue.
- Take a suggestion of what might be spoken and add it to the script. Read it aloud.
- Delete and rewrite words and punctuation to help the dialogue sound natural.

Revisiting and extending the stimulus

- Write the events in the form of Josie's diary written over a number of days. Alternatively, write the story as a series of letters, e-mails and messages exchanged between Josie and her Auntie Di.
- Imagine that Josie, Handra, Digger and Matt are the characters in a series of books or a television series. Write character descriptions and develop ideas for further stories. Each group could develop a different story plan.
- Help Josie not to make the same mistake again. Write detailed instructions for 'How to plan the perfect party'.
- Extend the story by role-playing situations only reported in the story (e.g. between Josie and her mother). Alternatively, role-play what happened next.

📖 Writer's Guide: Support for the Task

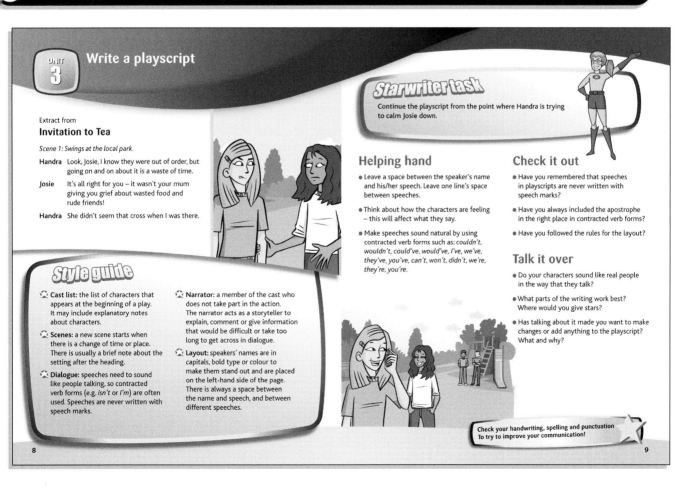

UNIT 3 Write a playscript

Starwriter task

Continue the playscript from the point where Handra is trying to calm Josie down.

Extract from
Invitation to Tea

Scene 1: Swings at the local park.

Handra Look, Josie, I know they were out of order, but going on and on about it is a waste of time.

Josie It's all right for you – it wasn't your mum giving you grief about wasted food and rude friends!

Handra She didn't seem that cross when I was there.

Helping hand

- Leave a space between the speaker's name and his/her speech. Leave one line's space between speeches.
- Think about how the characters are feeling – this will affect what they say.
- Make speeches sound natural by using contracted verb forms such as: *couldn't, wouldn't, could've, would've, I've, we've, they've, you've, can't, won't, didn't, we're, they're, you're.*

Check it out

- Have you remembered that speeches in playscripts are never written with speech marks?
- Have you always included the apostrophe in the right place in contracted verb forms?
- Have you followed the rules for the layout?

Talk it over

- Do your characters sound like real people in the way that they talk?
- What parts of the writing work best? Where would you give stars?
- Has talking about it made you want to make changes or add anything to the playscript? What and why?

Style guide

- ⭐ **Cast list:** the list of characters that appears at the beginning of a play. It may include explanatory notes about characters.
- ⭐ **Scenes:** a new scene starts when there is a change of time or place. There is usually a brief note about the setting after the heading.
- ⭐ **Dialogue:** speeches need to sound like people talking, so contracted verb forms (e.g. *isn't* or *I'm*) are often used. Speeches are never written with speech marks.
- ⭐ **Narrator:** a member of the cast who does not take part in the action. The narrator acts as a storyteller to explain, comment or give information that would be difficult or take too long to get across in dialogue.
- ⭐ **Layout:** speakers' names are in capitals, bold type or colour to make them stand out and are placed on the left-hand side of the page. There is always a space between the name and speech, and between different speeches.

Check your handwriting, spelling and punctuation To try to improve your communication!

8

9

25

Write a playscript

Assessing and Improving

Starwriter task	Continue the playscript from the point where Handra is trying to calm Josie down.
Learning intention	To use the standard conventions of playscripts.
Success criteria *Writer's Guide: 'Check it Out'*	• Have you remembered that speeches in playscripts are never written with speech marks? • Have you always put the apostrophe in the right place in contracted verb forms? • Have you followed the rules for layout?
Review with talk partner *Writer's Guide: 'Talk it Over'*	• Do your characters sound like real people in the way that they talk? • What parts of the writing work best? Where would you give stars? • Has talking about it made you want to make changes or add anything to the playscript? What and why?

? Children's Understanding of the Text Type

Main features

- Cast list: the characters are listed at the beginning of a playscript.
- Scenes: action taking place in a new setting or time is written as a new scene.
- Characters: the name of each character is written on the left-hand side of the script each time he or she speaks.
- Stage directions: instructions to characters about actions to take or how to speak are written inside brackets.
- Narrator: a non-acting member of the cast.

What is the difference between a playscript and a story?

- Both describe a situation or conflict and characters to an audience.
- Written or spoken stories tell the audience what happens through words. Plays show the audience what happens, using actors to perform the story.
- Playscripts tell the actors what to say and how to say it.
- Actors interpret the playscript to convey the plot to an audience.

Learning from the Writing Sample on the CD

Discuss and revise

- Read the script aloud. Ask the children to identify which speeches convey the characters' feelings. *Which words could be improved? How?* For example:
  - ○ add adverbs to describe how a character speaks
  - ○ alter a speech so the words convey the character's feelings, rather than using adverbs
  - ○ use contracted verbs to make the dialogue sound more natural
  - ○ add questions, exclamations, short sentences or ellipses to show expression.
- *Does the playscript reflect the original story?*

Grammar, spelling, punctuation and layout

- Ask the children to read the script with a partner. *Is it easy to follow? Is it set out like a playscript? How could it be improved?* For example, add stage directions in italics to convey an action.
- *Do the speeches sound natural?* Discuss how the punctuation can help the actor understand how to interpret the speech.
- *Is punctuation used correctly here?* Discuss the use of exclamation marks and capitalisation.
- *Are all words spelled correctly?*

Key Vocabulary

playscript	dialogue
cast	narrator
stage direction	speech

Annotate a playscript

Planning and Teaching

Text type	Playscript annotations
Literacy objective	To annotate a section of playscript as a preparation for performance, taking into account pace, movement, gesture and delivery of lines and the needs of the audience. To evaluate the script and the performance for their dramatic interest and impact.
Starwriter task	Choose a section of your playscript and add stage directions and annotations.
Suggestions for differentiation	▲ Add stage directions and annotations to your playscript to help the actors prepare for a performance. ▼ Work with a friend to add more stage directions and notes to the first part of the playscript.

Using the CD

Stimulus description

- A review of the story from the previous unit.
- The male Starwriter character appears on screen to add stage direction to the scene.
- Animation of actor adding annotation to the script.
- Animation of the scene acted on stage.

Using the Starwriter stimulus

- Remind children of the work in Unit 3, where they wrote the dialogue for the script. Explain that this time they will add stage directions and prepare the script for performance.
- Watch the stimulus. *What are the similarities and differences between the stage directions added by the writer and those written by the actors?*
- Show the text. Ask the children to identify stage directions. Highlight information about movements in one colour and those describing actions in a different colour.
- Discuss stage directions telling actors how to speak lines. Highlight one of Handra's lines and attach a thought bubble to it. *What is Handra thinking or feeling? How could you show this in your voice if you were playing the part?* Ask the children to suggest adverbs for the line of dialogue.
- Show the picture of the scene being acted out. Ask the children to imagine that they are the director. *What directions would you give to the actors?* Attach speech bubbles to record suggestions.
- Use sticky notes to practise writing stage directions and script annotations in the appropriate style.
- Show the stimulus again, this time with the children's scripts handy. Watch the directions added by Starwriter; then ask the children to work with a partner to add similar stage directions to their script. Show the actor playing Josie adding the annotation. Ask the children to add a similar annotation to their scripts.

Using Shared Writing

The Shared Writing section uses the annotated version of the playscript to demonstrate how to add stage directions and annotate a script.

- Highlight the stage directions. Discuss how they help the actor interpret the words.
- Take suggestions of other ways the dialogue could be spoken and of actions or expressions the actors would make. Use a different-sized font or colour and annotate the dialogue.
- Delete unnecessary words to make the annotations as brief notes.

Revisiting and extending the stimulus

- Imagine the play is to be performed on radio rather than on stage. Make changes to your script. Think about which stage directions might not be needed and what might need to be added (e.g. sound effects).
- Create a storyboard to turn the scene into a scene for film or TV. Plan a sequence of shots and show the camera angles you might use. Add notes to your storyboard about location, lighting and music.
- Imagine you have just been to see the play *Invitation to Tea*. Write a review of the play, commenting on both the script and the actors' performances.

📖 Writer's Guide: Support for the Task

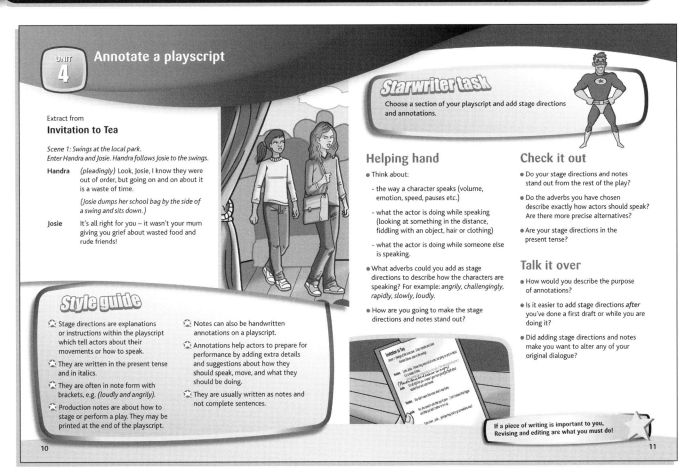

Assessing and Improving

Starwriter task	Choose a section of your playscript and add stage directions and annotations.
Learning intention	To annotate a playscript to help actors/readers.
Success criteria *Writer's Guide: 'Check it Out'*	• Do your stage directions and notes stand out from the rest of the play? • Do the adverbs you have chosen describe exactly how actors should speak? Are there more precise alternatives? • Are your stage directions in the present tense?
Review with talk partner *Writer's Guide: 'Talk it Over'*	• How would you describe the purpose of annotations? • Is it easier to add stage directions *after* you've done a first draft or while you are doing it? • Did adding stage directions and notes make you want to alter any of your original dialogue?

? Children's Understanding of the Text Type

Main features

- Cast list: the characters are listed at the beginning of a playscript.
- Scenes: action taking place in a new setting or time is written as a new scene.
- Characters: the name of each character is written on the left-hand side of the script each time he or she speaks.
- Stage directions: instructions to characters about actions to take or how to speak are written inside brackets.
- Narrator: a non-acting member of the cast.

Why are playscripts annotated?

- Playscripts tell the actors what to say and how to say it. Actors interpret the playscript to convey the plot to an audience.
- Playscripts can be annotated by the director and the actors.
- Annotations tell the actor how to interpret the lines of the script or the stage directions.
- They are handwritten onto the script and may use different colours and effects.
- Annotations are written as briefly as possible: they are not usually complete sentences.
- Stage directions are usually written by the author of the play. They are usually written in italics and within brackets.
- Stage directions can be added by the director and the actors to help them interpret the author's intentions.

Learning from the Writing Sample on the CD

Discuss and revise

- Ask the children to identify which annotations are good examples and explain why. *How could they be improved?* For example:
  - change pen colour to identify different ways of speaking lines
  - choose more accurate adverbs to describe speech
  - underline or circle directions showing action or movement
  - delete unnecessary words.

Grammar, spelling, punctuation and layout

- Ask the children who the annotations are intended for. *Does this affect the way the script is annotated? Is standard English necessary?*
- Identify and add punctuation marks which could help the actor interpret the annotations. For example, add exclamation marks to indicate word emphasis.
- Look at the layout of the annotations. *Would they be easy for an actor to follow?*
- *Is punctuation used correctly?* Ask the children to highlight where words and annotations are spelled incorrectly.

Key Vocabulary

playscript	director
stage direction	author
annotation	italic

Write a new myth

Planning and Teaching

Text type	Myth
Literacy objective	To write own versions of legends, myths and fables.
Starwriter task	Make a detailed plan or storyboard for the myth and write the last part of your story including an effective ending. Use a similar style to the opening of *Why Dragons Breathe Fire*.
Suggestions for differentiation	▲ Plan and write the myth to explain why dragons breathe fire in the same style as the opening. ▼ Make a plan for the myth *Why Dragons Breathe Fire*. Use the plan to help you tell the story to the group. Practise telling your story before you share it.

Using the CD

Stimulus description

- Title page and story opening of a myth called *Why Dragons Breathe Fire* appears on screen.
- An animation depicting the scene appears on screen.
- Children are prompted to decide for themselves how the story continues.

Using the Starwriter stimulus

- Pause the opening title page to discuss stories about dragons. *What do you know about dragons? How do they usually behave in traditional stories?*
- Play the stimulus. Discuss the prompts about how the story might continue. Attach thought bubbles around the scroll and type 'Perhaps' in each bubble: encourage the children to 'think, pair and share' ideas.
- Rewind to the image of the village and pause. Type 'What if ... ' ideas into thought bubbles placed around the image (e.g. What if the lava erupts into the village? What if the people upset the dragons?) Encourage the children to explore these ideas. *'Fast forward' in your head. What might happen as a result of these events? How would it explain why dragons breathe fire?*
- Show the text extract. Highlight and discuss some key features of myths, such as time connectives (e.g. 'long ago'), use of past tense, supernatural elements.
- Show the animation. Ask the children to focus on details about the setting. *Step into this world. What do you notice about the dragons, the volcano, the town? How would you make the scene sound peaceful? How would you make it sound threatening?* Use sticky notes and labels to add descriptive details about the dragons and the setting.
- Before the children begin to write, play the audio of the story opening again. Encourage the children to keep the 'storyteller's voice' in their head as they write.

Using Shared Writing

The Shared Writing section shows the opening paragraph of the myth for continuing.

- Add bullet-pointed notes to plan how the story will continue.
- Discuss the story ending. Brainstorm connective phrases that signal the conclusion of the story and add to the plan.
- Highlight 'storyteller' language in the original paragraph. Add concluding sentences that could be used to close the myth (e.g. 'And that is why … ').

Revisiting and extending the stimulus

- Imagine you are a news reporter. Write a report for either a television news programme or a newspaper (e.g. 'Today's headlines: Fire-breathing dragons threaten village').
- Use the animation as the stimulus for writing a descriptive poem about dragons, using adjectives, powerful verbs, similes and metaphors.
- Imagine that the animation is a trailer for a new film. Write an exciting voiceover to promote the film.
- Imagine the animation is part of a wildlife documentary on one of the last few surviving dragons. Write the script or a non-chronological report on dragons, giving details about their characteristics and habitat.

Writer's Guide: Support for the Task

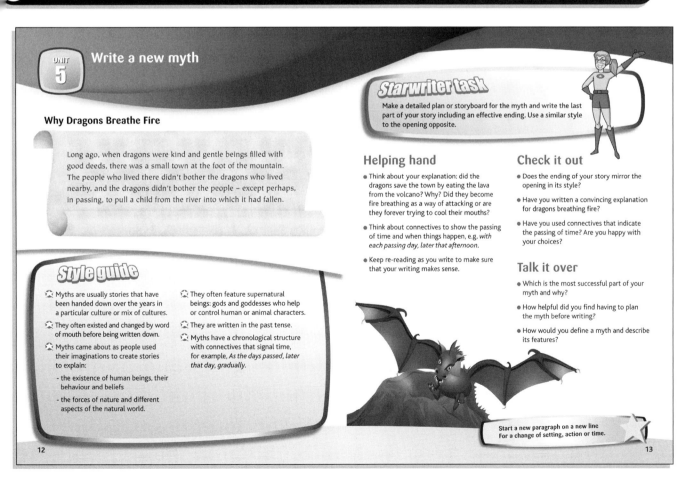

UNIT 5 — Write a new myth

Why Dragons Breathe Fire

Long ago, when dragons were kind and gentle beings filled with good deeds, there was a small town at the foot of the mountain. The people who lived there didn't bother the dragons who lived nearby, and the dragons didn't bother the people – except perhaps, in passing, to pull a child from the river into which it had fallen.

Style guide

- Myths are usually stories that have been handed down over the years in a particular culture or mix of cultures.
- They often existed and changed by word of mouth before being written down.
- Myths came about as people used their imaginations to create stories to explain:
  - the existence of human beings, their behaviour and beliefs
  - the forces of nature and different aspects of the natural world.
- They often feature supernatural beings: gods and goddesses who help or control human or animal characters.
- They are written in the past tense.
- Myths have a chronological structure with connectives that signal time, for example, *As the days passed, later that day, gradually.*

Starwriter task

Make a detailed plan or storyboard for the myth and write the last part of your story including an effective ending. Use a similar style to the opening opposite.

Helping hand

- Think about your explanation: did the dragons save the town by eating the lava from the volcano? Why? Did they become fire breathing as a way of attacking or are they forever trying to cool their mouths?
- Think about connectives to show the passing of time and when things happen, e.g. *with each passing day, later that afternoon.*
- Keep re-reading as you write to make sure that your writing makes sense.

Check it out

- Does the ending of your story mirror the opening in its style?
- Have you written a convincing explanation for dragons breathing fire?
- Have you used connectives that indicate the passing of time? Are you happy with your choices?

Talk it over

- Which is the most successful part of your myth and why?
- How helpful did you find having to plan the myth before writing?
- How would you define a myth and describe its features?

Start a new paragraph on a new line
For a change of setting, action or time.

12   13

Assessing and Improving

Starwriter task	Make a detailed plan or storyboard for the myth and write the last part of your story including an effective ending. Use a similar style to the opening of *Why Dragons Breathe Fire*.
Learning intention	To write the ending of the myth in the style of the opening.
Success criteria *Writer's Guide: 'Check it Out'*	• Does the ending of your story mirror the opening in its style? • Have you written a convincing explanation for dragons breathing fire? • Have you used connectives that indicate the passing of time? Are you happy with your choices?
Review with talk partner *Writer's Guide: 'Talk it Over'*	• Which is the most successful part of your myth and why? • How helpful did you find having to plan the myth before writing? • How would you define a myth and describe its features?

? Children's Understanding of the Text Type

Main features

- Myths are based in the past and are written using past-tense verbs.
- Characters include ordinary people and supernatural beings.
- Myths usually explain how something came to be or why something happens.
- They often include dramatic events or heroic behaviour.
- Myths originated as oral stories and were passed down by storytellers.
- The language of myths usually addresses the reader directly in order to give an explanation, using a 'storyteller voice'.
- Myths describe a sequence of events in chronological order.
- They use connectives to convey the passage of time, such as 'Long, long ago', 'Before', 'When at last', 'Eventually' and 'Later'.

Learning from the Writing Sample on the CD

Discuss and revise

- Read the storyboard aloud. *Do the events link together? Do you know where and when each event takes place? Are any parts of the story confusing? How could they be improved?* For example:
  - ○ add any missing events
  - ○ add paragraph breaks to show the start of each new event
  - ○ add a connecting phrase to the start of each paragraph to show when the new event happened.

- Read the ending aloud. *Is the explanation of why dragons breathe fire convincing? Is the style of the ending consistent with the style of the opening? What sounds good? What could be improved? How?* For example:
  - ○ use appropriate connectives
  - ○ add words for effect such as adjectives, powerful verbs or similes
  - ○ add an ellipsis or a dash for an intriguing pause
  - ○ form complex sentences to improve the flow
  - ○ add repetition of words and phrases for dramatic effect
  - ○ add a coda or comment to the end (e.g. 'From that time on ... ', 'And still to this day ... ').

Grammar, spelling, punctuation and layout

- Ask the children to identify descriptive words and phrases that best convey the setting and mood of the story and to say why they work. *How could they be improved?* For example:
  - ○ add expressive adjectives
  - ○ change the order of words and phrases
  - ○ include words linked to the senses
  - ○ change weak verbs for more powerful ones.

Key Vocabulary

myth	hero	event
story opening	connective	sequential
story ending	setting	voice
explanation	problem	

Use the structure to extend a classic poem

Planning and Teaching

Text type	Classic poem
Literacy objective	To use the structures of poems read to write extensions based on these, e.g. additional verses, or substituting own words and ideas.
Starwriter task	Extend the poem by two or three verses at the end that explain what the person is doing in the wood, who is watching and whether or not it is an echo or someone else calling out.
Suggestions for differentiation	▲ Extend the poem by writing additional stanzas at the beginning and end to create a context and explain what is going on.
	▼ Write a final verse for the poem in which the poet begins by saying, 'I care, I care!' and goes on to explain that he or she is searching for a lost love.

Using the CD

Stimulus description

- An animation accompanies the reading of 'Echo' by Walter de la Mare.
- Text of the poem appears on screen.
- Animation continues to encourage the children to extend the poem.

Using the Starwriter stimulus

- Select 'Screen Off' and play audio only. Ask the children to visualise the scene described in the poem and 'think, pair and share' ideas.
- Return to the start and select 'Screen On'. *How do the images capture the poem's mood? How do they extend your thinking about the poem?*
- Ask the children to suggest three 'facts' about events in the poem and three mysteries or questions. Record some of the mysteries and questions in thought bubbles around the image.
- Show the text of the poem. Encourage the children to read it aloud, conveying mood through expression, pace and tone. *What are your favourite phrases?* Highlight these. *Why are they effective?* Discuss use of adjectives, verbs and personification.
- Use the pencil and label tools to annotate the structure and form (e.g. link rhyming words, label the number of lines, underline repetition). Use the hide/reveal text tool to cover words and phrases. Ask the children to suggest new words that fit the rhyme, rhythm and structure.
- Discuss how the poem might continue. Use speech bubbles to record suggestions on screen.
- As the children work on their poems, play the audio to help them keep the sound and mood of the poem in their heads.
- Read the completed poems over the animation with sound effects in the last section of the stimulus.

Using Shared Writing

The Shared Writing section uses the last verse as a model for continuing the poem, using the same rhythm and rhyme scheme.

- Identify the rhythm of the poem. Highlight the rhyming words.
- Add the first two lines of a new verse. Hide words that do not fit the rhythm of the original and take suggestions to improve the rhythm.
- Highlight the last word of the second new line and make a list of suggestions that will continue the rhyme.

Revisiting and extending the stimulus

- Imagine the animation was the opening scene of a film. *What sort of film would it be? A mystery, an adventure? Why?* Create a storyboard to show how the scene might develop, building up the sense of suspense. Include notes about actions, sounds, lighting and camera angles.
- Develop a character profile for the person in the poem. *Who is this person? Where do they come from? What three things stand out about them? What is their secret or problem?* Write a paragraph about the character before they entered the wood.
- Imagine you are the person in the wood. Write about your experience in your diary.

Writer's Guide: Support for the Task

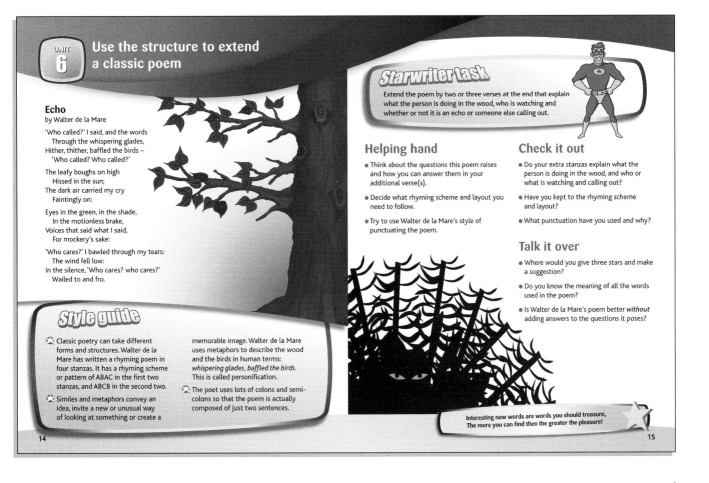

UNIT 6

Use the structure to extend a classic poem

Echo
by Walter de la Mare

'Who called?' I said, and the words
  Through the whispering glades,
Hither, thither, baffled the birds –
  'Who called? Who called?'

The leafy boughs on high
  Hissed in the sun;
The dark air carried my cry
  Faintingly on:

Eyes in the green, in the shade,
  In the motionless brake,
Voices that said what I said,
  For mockery's sake:

'Who cares?' I bawled through my tears:
  The wind fell low:
In the silence, 'Who cares? who cares?'
  Wailed to and fro.

Style guide

- Classic poetry can take different forms and structures. Walter de la Mare has written a rhyming poem in four stanzas. It has a rhyming scheme or pattern of ABAC in the first two stanzas, and ABCB in the second two.
- Similes and metaphors convey an idea, invite a new or unusual way of looking at something or create a memorable image. Walter de la Mare uses metaphors to describe the wood and the birds in human terms: *whispering glades, baffled the birds*. This is called personification.
- The poet uses lots of colons and semi-colons so that the poem is actually composed of just two sentences.

Starwriter task

Extend the poem by two or three verses at the end that explain what the person is doing in the wood, who is watching and whether or not it is an echo or someone else calling out.

Helping hand

- Think about the questions this poem raises and how you can answer them in your additional verse(s).
- Decide what rhyming scheme and layout you need to follow.
- Try to use Walter de la Mare's style of punctuating the poem.

Check it out

- Do your extra stanzas explain what the person is doing in the wood, and who or what is watching and calling out?
- Have you kept to the rhyming scheme and layout?
- What punctuation have you used and why?

Talk it over

- Where would you give three stars and make a suggestion?
- Do you know the meaning of all the words used in the poem?
- Is Walter de la Mare's poem better *without* adding answers to the questions it poses?

Interesting new words are words you should treasure,
The more you can find then the greater the pleasure!

14

15

Use the structure to extend a classic poem

Assessing and Improving

Starwriter task	Extend the poem by two or three verses at the end that explain what the person is doing in the wood, who is watching and whether or not it is an echo or someone else calling out.
Learning intention	To use the structure of the poem to write additional verses.
Success criteria *Writer's Guide: 'Check it Out'*	• Do your extra stanzas explain what the person is doing in the wood and who or what is watching and calling out? • Have you kept to the rhyming scheme and layout? • What punctuation have you used and why?
Review with talk partner *Writer's Guide: 'Talk it Over'*	• Where would you give three stars and make a suggestion? • Do you know the meaning of all the words used in the poem? • Is Walter de la Mare's poem better *without* adding answers to the questions it poses?

? Children's Understanding of the Text Type

Main features

• Classic poetry follows a layout and rhyme scheme and usually adheres to it throughout the poem.

• There are many different forms and structures in classic poetry.

• Classic poems use literary devices to good effect. Imagery, metaphor and personification are often used.

• The sounds of the words are as important as their meanings.

• Classic poetry has been written by poets who are established, historically, as leaders of their craft.

Learning from the Writing Sample on the CD

Discuss and revise

- Read the verses aloud. *Does it look and sound like the original poem? What needs to be improved? How could it be improved?* For example:
  - ○ check that the rhyme scheme in the new verses is the same as the poet's
  - ○ look at the line breaks. *Does each verse have four lines?*
  - ○ re-order words or cut words to help the rhythm
  - ○ replace obvious ideas with something more unusual
  - ○ change a simile into a metaphor.
- *Do the new verses tell us who is in the wood, or whether or not it is an echo?*
  - ○ add some words that describe objects or creatures in the woods as if they were human
  - ○ add extra verses to offer explanations.

Grammar, spelling, punctuation and layout

- *How could the punctuation and layout be improved to be a better match to the original poem?* For example:
  - ○ experiment with punctuation by adding colons and semi-colons to rewrite the verses as one continuous sentence.

Key Vocabulary

rhyme	verse	metaphor
rhythm	form	personification
stanza	structure	

Planning and Teaching

Text type	Poem (revise and edit)
Literacy objective	To review and edit writing to produce a final form, matched to the needs of an identified reader.
Starwriter task	Choose a poem that you have written. Discuss with a friend anything you think could be improved. Work alone to revise your poem.
Suggestions for differentiation	▲ Go through a poem you have written and highlight anything you think could be improved. Revise and edit your poem.
	▼ Choose a poem you have written. Go through it with a friend and underline anything you think could be improved. Discuss how you could make changes.

⊙ Using the CD

Stimulus description

- The Starwriter character appears on screen, presenting his advice on revising and editing a poem through points, poems and animations.
- 'Before' and 'after' poems appear on screen for comparison.

Using the Starwriter stimulus

- Discuss the terms 'revising' and 'editing'. *Why do we need to revise and edit a poem?*
- Show the stimulus. *What are Starwriter's top tips on polishing poetry? Which tip is your 'number one'?*
- Show each of Starwriter's points on screen. *What does Starwriter mean? Can you give me some examples?* Use a sticky note or a speech bubble to add examples of 'best words', similes and metaphors or problems to check out.
- Show 'Using similes and metaphors is like salt ... '. Encourage the children to suggest their own 'writing similes' (e.g. 'Finding the best word is like ... ', 'Polishing a poem is like ... '). Record these on screen in thought bubbles.
- Pause on the 'after' poem. Attach a thought bubble to an amendment to prompt discussion of why the poet made the changes. *What was the author thinking? This line is better because ...*
- Show the stimulus again, pausing to focus on each of Starwriter's points in turn. Ask the children to read through their poem with a writing partner and find one example to improve.

Using Shared Writing

The Shared Writing section features a badly-written poem for editing.

* Highlight the images, words and phrases that need improvement.
* Use the hide/reveal text tool to cover words and encourage children to suggest alternatives, explaining the effect they wish to achieve.

Revisiting and extending the stimulus

* Imagine you are writing a Starwriter page for your school magazine. This week's feature is on 'Polishing your poetry'. Plan and write the article using ideas from the stimulus.
* Write a story based on the Starwriter characters, two superheroes who step in to help children solve their writing problems.
* Write a poem or rap for the Starwriter characters to perform. It has to be on the theme of writing and it has to be fun.

Writer's Guide: Support for the Task

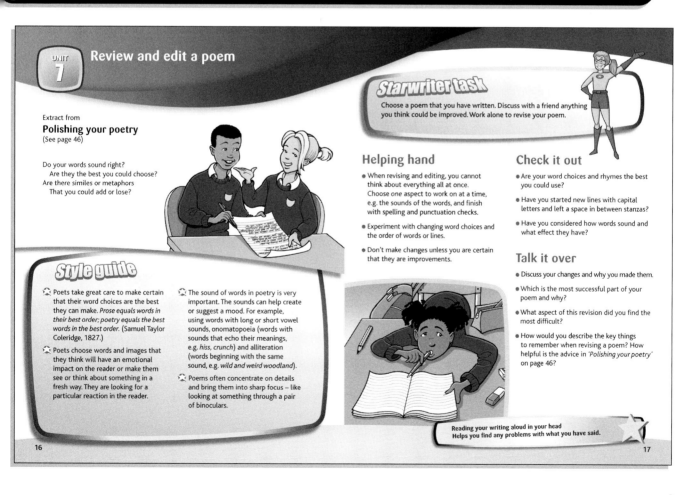

UNIT 7

Review and edit a poem

Starwriter task
Choose a poem that you have written. Discuss with a friend anything you think could be improved. Work alone to revise your poem.

Extract from
Polishing your poetry
(See page 46)

Do your words sound right?
　Are they the best you could choose?
Are there similes or metaphors
　That you could add or lose?

Helping hand
* When revising and editing, you cannot think about everything all at once. Choose *one* aspect to work on at a time, e.g. the sounds of the words, and finish with spelling and punctuation checks.
* Experiment with changing word choices and the order of words or lines.
* Don't make changes unless you are certain that they are improvements.

Check it out
* Are your word choices and rhymes the best you could use?
* Have you started new lines with capital letters and left a space in between stanzas?
* Have you considered how words sound and what effect they have?

Talk it over
* Discuss your changes and why you made them.
* Which is the most successful part of your poem and why?
* What aspect of this revision did you find the most difficult?
* How would you describe the key things to remember when revising a poem? How helpful is the advice in 'Polishing your poetry' on page 46?

Style guide
* Poets take great care to make certain that their word choices are the best they can make. *Prose equals words in their best order; poetry equals the best words in the best order.* (Samuel Taylor Coleridge, 1827.)
* Poets choose words and images that they think will have an emotional impact on the reader or make them see or think about something in a fresh way. They are looking for a particular reaction in the reader.
* The sound of words in poetry is very important. The sounds can help create or suggest a mood. For example, using words with long or short vowel sounds, onomatopoeia (words with sounds that echo their meanings, e.g. *hiss, crunch*) and alliteration (words beginning with the same sound, e.g. *wild and weird woodland*).
* Poems often concentrate on details and bring them into sharp focus – like looking at something through a pair of binoculars.

Reading your writing aloud in your head
Helps you find any problems with what you have said.

16　　　　　　17

Assessing and Improving

Starwriter task	Choose a poem that you have written. Discuss with a friend anything you think could be improved. Work alone to revise your poem.
Learning intention	To polish and improve a previously written poem.
Success criteria **Writer's Guide: 'Check it Out'**	• Are your word choices and rhymes the best you could use? • Have you started new lines with capital letters and left a space in between stanzas? • Have you considered how words sound and what effect they have?
Review with talk partner **Writer's Guide: 'Talk it Over'**	• Discuss your changes and why you made them. • Which is the most successful part of your poem and why? • What aspect of this revision did you find the most difficult? • How would you describe the key things to remember when revising a poem? How helpful is the advice in *'Polishing your poetry'*?

? Children's Understanding of the Text Type

Main features

- There are many different forms and structures in poetry.
- Imagery, metaphor and personification are often used.
- The sounds of the words are as important as their meanings.
- Each line of a poem usually – but not always – begins with a capital letter.
- Spaces usually occur between verses in classic forms of poetry.
- Rhythm and rhyme are important in certain poetic forms, for example, performance poetry.
- Repetition is often used for effect.

Learning from the Writing Sample on the CD

Discuss and revise

- Read both poems aloud. Highlight places where the first poem has been noticeably improved and discuss these.

- *How could the second poem still be improved?* For example:
  - use more expressive adjectives
  - replace weak verbs with more powerful ones
  - use adverbs to enhance verbs
  - replace any clichéd metaphors or similes
  - make the alliteration ('fir is as red as fire', etc.) stronger.
  - develop the personification by having the poem in one voice only
  - experiment with the order of the words.

Grammar, spelling, punctuation and layout

- Read the poems aloud. *Does the punctuation affect the sound or meaning of the poem?* Experiment with altering the punctuation. For example:
  - remove all punctuation to see how the poem sounds
  - insert commas, semi-colons and full stops to alter the length of a pause.

Key Vocabulary

rhyme	form	revision
rhythm	structure	edit
stanza	metaphor	polish
verse	personification	

Write an informal letter from a character

Planning and Teaching

Text type	Informal letter
Literacy objective	To write from another character's point of view, e.g. retelling an incident in letter form.
Starwriter task	Complete Hera's letter to her friend.
Suggestions for differentiation	▲ Write Hera's letter and write a short reply from Kore. ▼ Role-play Hera talking to her friend Kore and telling her what has happened. Then write the letter from Hera to Kore.

Using the CD

Stimulus description

- Animation of 'The Cuckoo's Trick' (a Greek myth retold by Lucy Coates) is shown.
- Hera, the main character in the story, appears on screen writing a letter.
- The start of the letter is zoomed-in on as a prompt for the children to continue it.

Using the Starwriter stimulus

- Show the story. Encourage the children to respond. *What do you think about Zeus and Hera? Why?*
- Read the letter aloud to establish the 'voice' of Hera. *How is the letter different from the story? How does it alter our view of events? What is Hera's view? What are her thoughts as she writes the letter?* Use thought bubbles to record Hera's thoughts and feelings around the image of her writing the letter.
- Show the text of the letter. Ask the children to highlight sentences or phrases that show it is a personal letter to a close friend.
- Return to the start of the stimulus and show the first part of the story again. Then click on the text tab to compare Hera's letter. *What details are in both the letter and the story? What has Hera added in her letter? Why?* Highlight details added for the benefit of Kore.
- Play the story again. Ask the children to make a note of the main sequence of events to help them plan their letter. Use sticky notes or labels to mark and name each new picture or stage of the story on screen (e.g. 1 Showered with gifts).
- Return to the start and show the sequence of images with audio off. Encourage the children to look at events through Hera's eyes. Ask them to work with a partner and orally rehearse Hera's version of events. *What details might she include? How will she say it?*
- Attach thought bubbles around the images of Hera to encourage the children to think about her feelings at different points. Attach speech bubbles around the image to encourage the children to say how she might comment on the events to her friend.

Using Shared Writing

The Shared Writing section features the beginning of a letter from Hera to Kore, relating how Zeus tricked Hera into marrying him.

- Make notes of details from the story that Hera would want to include in her letter.
- Add sentences to continue the letter. Read them aloud and change words and phrases to continue the personal tone.
- Highlight words that can be contracted into a conversational form.

Revisiting and extending the stimulus

- The story is going to be put on as a play. Develop dialogue for each scene and include notes for the actors.
- Imagine you are chief news reporter on the *Greek Herald*. It's your job to cover the wedding of Zeus and Hera. Watch and listen to the story and make notes to help you write your special report.
- Write an interview with Hera to appear in the top celebrity magazine *Star Gazer*. You will need to think of some good questions and decide how Hera would answer them.
- Use the sequence of pictures as the basis for an oral retelling of the story. Plan and rehearse the retelling a number of times, thinking about using expression, pauses and adding interesting details.

📖 Writer's Guide: Support for the Task

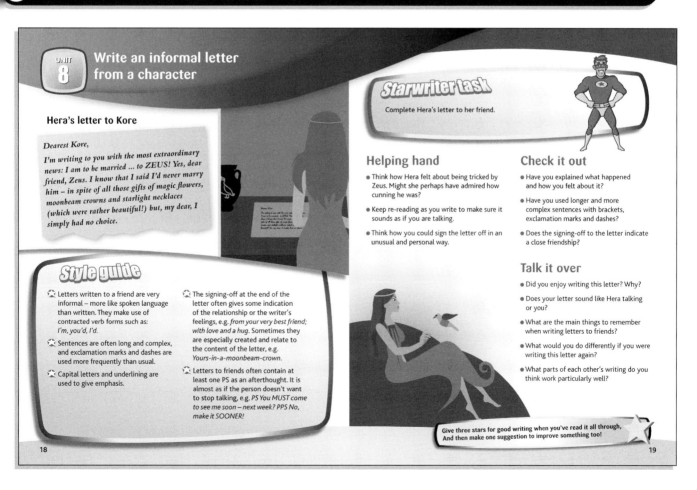

UNIT 8

Write an informal letter from a character

Starwriter task

Complete Hera's letter to her friend.

Hera's letter to Kore

Dearest Kore,

I'm writing to you with the most extraordinary news: I am to be married ... to ZEUS! Yes, dear friend, Zeus. I know that I said I'd never marry him – in spite of all those gifts of magic flowers, moonbeam crowns and starlight necklaces (which were rather beautiful!) but, my dear, I simply had no choice.

Helping hand

- Think how Hera felt about being tricked by Zeus. Might she perhaps have admired how cunning he was?
- Keep re-reading as you write to make sure it sounds as if you are talking.
- Think how you could sign the letter off in an unusual and personal way.

Check it out

- Have you explained what happened and how you felt about it?
- Have you used longer and more complex sentences with brackets, exclamation marks and dashes?
- Does the signing-off to the letter indicate a close friendship?

Talk it over

- Did you enjoy writing this letter? Why?
- Does your letter sound like Hera talking or you?
- What are the main things to remember when writing letters to friends?
- What would you do differently if you were writing this letter again?
- What parts of each other's writing do you think work particularly well?

Style guide

- ✂ Letters written to a friend are very informal – more like spoken language than written. They make use of contracted verb forms such as: I'm, you'd, I'd.
- ✂ Sentences are often long and complex, and exclamation marks and dashes are used more frequently than usual.
- ✂ Capital letters and underlining are used to give emphasis.

- ✂ The signing-off at the end of the letter often gives some indication of the relationship or the writer's feelings, e.g. *from your very best friend; with love and a hug*. Sometimes they are especially created and relate to the content of the letter, e.g. *Yours-in-a-moonbeam-crown.*
- ✂ Letters to friends often contain at least one PS as an afterthought. It is almost as if the person doesn't want to stop talking, e.g. *PS You MUST come to see me soon – next week? PPS No, make it SOONER!*

Give three stars for good writing when you've read it all through, And then make one suggestion to improve something too!

18   19

Assessing and Improving

Starwriter task	Complete Hera's letter to her friend.
Learning intention	To complete a letter, in role, in an informal style.
Success criteria *Writer's Guide: 'Check it Out'*	• Have you explained what happened and how you felt about it? • Have you used longer and more complex sentences with brackets, exclamation marks and dashes? • Does the signing-off to the letter indicate a close friendship?
Review with talk partner *Writer's Guide: 'Talk it Over'*	• Did you enjoy writing this letter? Why? • Does your letter sound like Hera talking or you? • What are the main things to remember when writing letters to friends? • What would you do differently if you were writing this letter again? • What parts of each other's writing do you think work particularly well?

❓ Children's Understanding of the Text Type

Main features

• Letters are written for a range of purposes, for example to inform, to complain, to persuade.

• All letters open with a greeting to the intended recipient. When the writer knows the recipient well, this greeting will be informal and may take a variety of forms (e.g. 'Dear ... ', 'Hi ... ' or 'How's it going?'), followed by the recipient's first name rather than Mr/Mrs or Sir/Madam.

• Informal letters do not have to follow the conventions of standard punctuation. Sentences are often long and use exclamation marks, dashes and brackets.

• Formal letters usually close with 'Yours faithfully' if they began with 'Dear Sir' or 'Yours sincerely' if they began with the recipient's name (e.g. 'Dear Mr Smith' or 'Dear Ben'). Informal letters close in a variety of ways, depending on the wishes and relationship of writer and recipient. This may be followed by an afterthought in the form of a PS.

Writing in character

• To make the letter appear authentic to the character, think about the following:
  ○ When did the character live? Is the vocabulary appropriate to the period?
  ○ What role and status does the character have?
  ○ What sort of personality is the character?
  ○ What is the character hoping to achieve by writing a letter?

Learning from the Writing Sample on the CD

Discuss and revise

- Read the letter aloud. *Does it sound like a chatty letter to a friend?* Ask the children to identify examples of this and say why they work. *Which words or phrases could be improved? How?* For example:
  - use longer sentences to give a conversational tone
  - add lively, descriptive detail and personal comments
  - add a personal and suitable signing-off.

Grammar, spelling, punctuation and layout

- Experiment with altering the paragraphs to have one or two longer paragraphs, and consider how this adds to or detracts from the informality.

- Experiment with formal and informal vocabulary.

- Highlight incorrect spelling and grammar. Discuss how unlike in texting, these should still be used correctly in an informal letter.

- *How does the writer use punctuation to show how the character is feeling? How else might we do this?* Experiment with changing punctuation to include dashes and underlining for emphasis.

Key Vocabulary

formal	colon	bracket
informal	semi-colon	opening greeting
signing-off	hyphen	parenthesis

Write additional dialogue

Planning and Teaching

Text type	Dialogue
Literacy objective	To write in the style of the author, e.g. writing additional dialogue.
Starwriter task	Write dialogue for the extract from *Little House in the Big Woods*.
Suggestions for differentiation	▲ Write dialogue for the extract and continue it, with linking sentences, to include the children making snow pictures. ▼ Write the dialogue for this part of the story: Alice said they must go outdoors to do it and Ma thought it was too cold for Laura to play outdoors. But when she saw how disappointed Laura was, she said she might go, after all, for a little while. Begin: Alice said, "We must … "

Using the CD

Stimulus description

- An illustrated extract from the story *Little House in the Big Woods* by Laura Ingalls Wilder is shown.
- A section of text from the book appears on screen with dialogue highlighted.
- Illustrated reading of story continues, to prompt the children to write additional dialogue.

Using the Starwriter stimulus

- Show the stimulus. Encourage the children to think about the characters and setting of the story. *Who are these characters? When and where did they live?*
- Show the image of inside the log cabin. Ask the children to look for clues about the life of the family. *Step into the picture. Have a good look around. What do you notice? How is their life different from yours?* Use labels and sticky notes to record details and vocabulary that might be useful when writing the dialogue.
- Show the text extract to focus on the use of dialogue. Ask the children to highlight examples of reported speech in one colour and direct speech in a different colour. Discuss the differences. Use the pencil tool to annotate features of direct speech: circle the speech marks; underline reporting clauses.
- Show the image of inside the log cabin again. Ask the children to add speech bubbles to show what the various characters are saying. Encourage them to use and develop ideas from the text.
- Show the image of outside the log cabin. Use thought bubbles to encourage the children to freeze-frame the scene and suggest what the characters are thinking and feeling. Type their ideas into the thought bubbles.
- Attach speech bubbles to the same image and discuss what each character might be saying.
- Discuss *how* they might say it. Use a sticky note to record suggestions for verbs and adverbs to use in place of 'said'.

Using Shared Writing

The Shared Writing section shows a descriptive paragraph, with the question 'What did they say?'.

- Highlight the characters' names to identify potential speakers.
- Discuss what might be said as Laura and Mary meet their aunt, uncle and cousins, and type in examples.
- Add reporting clauses and speech punctuation.

Revisiting and extending the stimulus

- Write a diary entry for one of the characters. Describe the day's events in the role of that character. Try imagining their life and extending the diary by writing about another day.
- Imagine you have been asked to help choose a story to be serialised on children's television. Would this be a good story to choose? Write a commentary giving your thoughts and opinions.
- Imagine you travel back in time to visit the family in the little house. Would you enjoy life there or would you hate it? Write a list of points for and against and then give your conclusion.
- Build up a character dossier for one the characters in the story. Use headings such as name, age, relationship to other characters, physical appearance and personality. Use your imagination to fill in any gaps.

Writer's Guide: Support for the Task

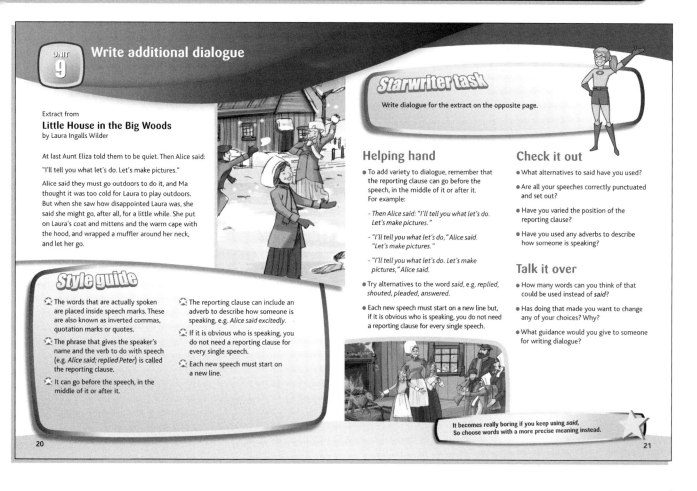

UNIT 9

Write additional dialogue

Extract from
Little House in the Big Woods
by Laura Ingalls Wilder

At last Aunt Eliza told them to be quiet. Then Alice said:

"I'll tell you what let's do. Let's make pictures."

Alice said they must go outdoors to do it, and Ma thought it was too cold for Laura to play outdoors. But when she saw how disappointed Laura was, she said she might go, after all, for a little while. She put on Laura's coat and mittens and the warm cape with the hood, and wrapped a muffler around her neck, and let her go.

Style guide

- The words that are actually spoken are placed inside speech marks. These are also known as inverted commas, quotation marks or quotes.
- The phrase that gives the speaker's name and the verb to do with speech (e.g. *Alice said; replied Peter*) is called the reporting clause.
- It can go before the speech, in the middle of it or after it.
- The reporting clause can include an adverb to describe how someone is speaking, e.g. *Alice said excitedly.*
- If it is obvious who is speaking, you do not need a reporting clause for every single speech.
- Each new speech must start on a new line.

Starwriter task

Write dialogue for the extract on the opposite page.

Helping hand

- To add variety to dialogue, remember that the reporting clause can go before the speech, in the middle of it or after it. For example:
  - *Then Alice said: "I'll tell you what let's do. Let's make pictures."*
  - *"I'll tell you what let's do," Alice said. "Let's make pictures."*
  - *"I'll tell you what let's do. Let's make pictures," Alice said.*
- Try alternatives to the word *said*, e.g. *replied, shouted, pleaded, answered.*
- Each new speech must start on a new line but, if it is obvious who is speaking, you do not need a reporting clause for every single speech.

Check it out

- What alternatives to said have you used?
- Are all your speeches correctly punctuated and set out?
- Have you varied the position of the reporting clause?
- Have you used any adverbs to describe how someone is speaking?

Talk it over

- How many words can you think of that could be used instead of *said*?
- Has doing that made you want to change any of your choices? Why?
- What guidance would you give to someone for writing dialogue?

It becomes really boring if you keep using *said*,
So choose words with a more precise meaning instead.

20

21

Write additional dialogue

Assessing and Improving

Starwriter task	Write dialogue for the extract from *Little House in the Big Woods*.
Learning intention	To turn reported speech into dialogue.
Success criteria *Writer's Guide: 'Check it Out'*	• What alternatives to *said* have you used? • Are all your speeches correctly punctuated and set out? • Have you varied the position of the reporting clause? • Have you used any adverbs to describe how someone is speaking?
Review with talk partner *Writer's Guide: 'Talk it Over'*	• How many words can you think of that could be used instead of *said*? • Has doing that made you want to change any of your choices? Why? • What guidance would you give to someone for writing dialogue?

? Children's Understanding of the Text Type

Main features

- Direct speech is always written inside speech marks (e.g. "I am going home," he said).
- Reported speech does not need speech marks (e.g. He said he was going home or He told them he was going home).
- The reporting clause tells readers how the words are spoken. It can come at the beginning, in the middle or at the end of the spoken words.
- Punctuation of the spoken words is always contained within the speech marks.
- New speech is always written on a new line.

What is special about writing dialogue?

- Dialogue can let readers know about a character's motives and feelings.
- It allows characters to tell readers about the plot.
- Dialogue allows characters to set the tone or mood.
- It can give readers a sense of the setting.
- Dialogue breaks up the page and leads the reader's eye onwards.

Learning from the Writing Sample on the CD

Discuss and revise

- Read the dialogue aloud. *Does it read well?* Ask the children to identify examples and say why they work. *Which parts could be improved? How?* For example:
  - use more alternatives to 'said'
  - vary the position of the reporting clause
  - check that the reporting clause is necessary
  - make the spoken words sound realistic and natural.

- *Would some direct speech work better as reported speech?* Experiment with changing direct speech to reported.

- Experiment with using strong, interesting words and phrases.

- *Is the dialogue appropriate to the characters and the setting? Is it appropriate to the historical period of the story? What needs to be changed?* For example:
  - remove any modern-day vocabulary
  - add some words and phrases from the original extract.

- Read the dialogue aloud with expression. *Does it work?*

Grammar, spelling, punctuation and layout

- *Has the dialogue been punctuated and set out appropriately? How could it be improved?* For example:
  - ensure all sentences begin with a capital letter and end with a full stop
  - write all direct speech inside speech marks
  - conclude spoken words with a comma to separate words spoken from the reporting clause
  - conclude spoken words with a full stop when the reporting clause precedes the speech
  - ensure that all punctuation, such as question marks or exclamation marks, is included inside the speech marks.

- *Is the spelling correct?* Ask the children to highlight errors.

Key Vocabulary

speech mark	reporting clause
quotation mark	powerful verb
dialogue	

Comment on a story

Planning and Teaching

Text type	Story commentary
Literacy objective	To write discursively about a novel or story, e.g. to describe, explain or comment on it.
Starwriter task	Write a commentary on *The Little Match Girl*. Include a paragraph on the message of the story.
Suggestions for differentiation	▲ Write about *The Little Match Girl*. Find and read the original version and include a comparison of the two in your commentary. ▼ Write about *The Little Match Girl*. In particular, think about the girl, what kind of life she has and whether or not her death is an escape for her.

Using the CD

Stimulus description

- An animated reading of the story *The Little Match Girl* is shown.
- Images from the story and a prompt appear on screen to encourage the children to think about the story before writing a commentary.

Using the Starwriter stimulus

- Show the story. Pause on the final image and ask the children to 'pair and share' initial thoughts. *What is your reaction? How does the story make you feel? Why?* Add some of the comments in thought bubbles.
- Discuss what a commentary might include. *What should we comment on?* (e.g. the character of the girl, the build-up and ending of the story, the theme/ message.) Record suggestions on sticky notes.
- Return to the start and show the story again. Ask the children to this time make notes on their individual whiteboards of details to refer to when writing their commentary. Use sticky notes or labels to mark each new image or development in the story so it is easy to return to a particular part of the story in later discussion.
- Re-read the suggestions you recorded on sticky notes earlier. Use them to encourage further discussion (e.g. *What did you think about the plot? What makes you say that?*).
- Encourage the children to justify their comments by using the markers to go back and find the relevant part of the story. Use sticky notes to record on screen references to the story that could be used in their commentary.
- Show the text of the story and use the highlighter to mark phrases or sentences that could be quoted in the commentary to support ideas.
- Discuss the need to use an impersonal style in the commentary. Go back to the images where some of the children's personal comments have been recorded in thought bubbles. Discuss how to write these in a more formal style.

Using Shared Writing

The Shared Writing section shows a list of questions to help the children write a commentary on the story of *The Little Match Girl*.

- Make brief notes to answer the questions.
- Discuss features of commentaries (see page 54).
- Model reworking the notes into formal sentences for the children to use in their commentaries.

Revisiting and extending the stimulus

- Use the stimulus as a historical resource. What does it tell us about the life of a poor child in Victorian Britain? Make notes from the story and from other sources and use the information to write a report.
- Use the images to persuade a Victorian audience that something must be done to improve the lives of street children. Write a persuasive argument to accompany the pictures.
- Use the stimulus to develop ideas for a hot-seating activity, thinking of questions to ask the girl in the story and role-playing how she might answer.
- Write an additional event for the story, for example a meeting with another character. Remember to keep to the style of the original story.

📖 Writer's Guide: Support for the Task

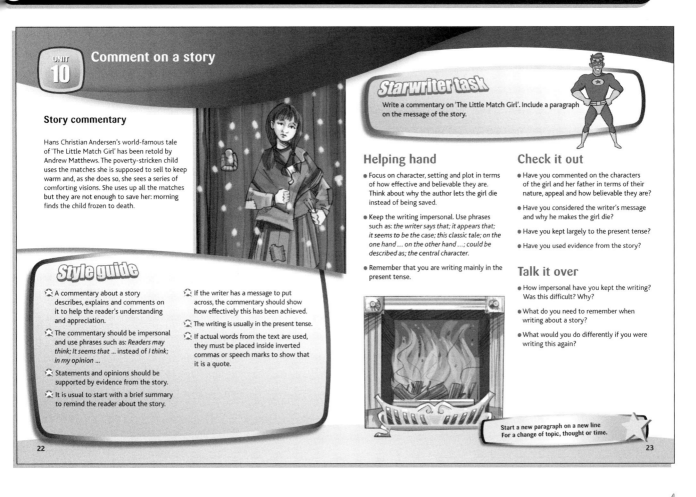

UNIT 10

Comment on a story

Story commentary

Hans Christian Andersen's world-famous tale of 'The Little Match Girl' has been retold by Andrew Matthews. The poverty-stricken child uses the matches she is supposed to sell to keep warm and, as she does so, she sees a series of comforting visions. She uses up all the matches but they are not enough to save her: morning finds the child frozen to death.

Style guide

- ☆ A commentary about a story describes, explains and comments on it to help the reader's understanding and appreciation.
- ☆ The commentary should be impersonal and use phrases such as: *Readers may think*; *It seems that ...* instead of *I think*; *in my opinion ...*
- ☆ Statements and opinions should be supported by evidence from the story.
- ☆ It is usual to start with a brief summary to remind the reader about the story.
- ☆ If the writer has a message to put across, the commentary should show how effectively this has been achieved.
- ☆ The writing is usually in the present tense.
- ☆ If actual words from the text are used, they must be placed inside inverted commas or speech marks to show that it is a quote.

Starwriter task

Write a commentary on 'The Little Match Girl'. Include a paragraph on the message of the story.

Helping hand

- Focus on character, setting and plot in terms of how effective and believable they are. Think about why the author lets the girl die instead of being saved.
- Keep the writing impersonal. Use phrases such as: *the writer says that*; *it appears that*; *it seems to be the case*; *this classic tale*; *on the one hand ... on the other hand ...*; *could be described as*; *the central character.*
- Remember that you are writing mainly in the present tense.

Check it out

- Have you commented on the characters of the girl and her father in terms of their nature, appeal and how believable they are?
- Have you considered the writer's message and why he makes the girl die?
- Have you kept largely to the present tense?
- Have you used evidence from the story?

Talk it over

- How impersonal have you kept the writing? Was this difficult? Why?
- What do you need to remember when writing about a story?
- What would you do differently if you were writing this again?

Start a new paragraph on a new line. For a change of topic, thought or time.

22   23

Assessing and Improving

Starwriter task	Write a commentary on *The Little Match Girl.* Include a paragraph on the message of the story.
Learning intention	To write a story commentary in an impersonal style.
Success criteria ***Writer's Guide: 'Check it Out'***	• Have you commented on the characters of the girl and her father in terms of their nature, appeal and how believable they are? • Have you considered the writer's message and why he makes the girl die? • Have you kept largely to the present tense? • Have you used evidence from the story?
Review with talk partner ***Writer's Guide: 'Talk it Over'***	• How impersonal have you kept the writing? Was this difficult? Why? • What do you need to remember when writing about a story? • What would you do differently if you were writing this again?

? Children's Understanding of the Text Type

Main features

- A commentary is written to help readers understand and appreciate a text.
- It is impartial so it does not provide the writer's personal opinions.
- A story commentary will often begin with a summary of the plot to remind the readers of the key events.
- A commentary is usually written in the present tense.
- A commentary can give background information about the author or subject to help explain the text further.
- It may explain the author's intention in the story.
- Statements and opinions in a commentary will be supported by evidence from the story itself.
- A commentary often contains direct quotes from the story.

Learning from the Writing Sample on the CD

Discuss and revise

- Ask the children to identify successful features of the commentary and say why they work. *Does it maintain an impersonal style? Which words or phrases could be improved? How?* For example:
  - ○ change active verb phrases to passive verb phrases
  - ○ support comments with evidence
  - ○ write evidence from the story in quotation marks
  - ○ use the present tense consistently
  - ○ use strong, interesting words
  - ○ use a variety of connectives to improve the fluency of reading.

- Ask the children to identify sentences, phrases or points made in the commentary that actually help their understanding of the story.

- *Does the commentary help to explain each element of the story? How could this be improved?*
  For example:
  - ○ discuss the characters of the father and grandmother in more detail
  - ○ add examples or evidence from the text to back up points made
  - ○ add a reason to explain a point.

- *Does the commentary give a believable reason for the author's choice of ending? If so, why is it believable?*

Grammar, spelling, punctuation and layout

- *Has an impersonal tone and passive language been used?*
- *Are quotations from the story punctuated with speech marks?*
- Check the layout of the commentary. *Have paragraphs been used for introducing new points?*
- Experiment with using different connectives to link points made.
- *Is the spelling correct?*

Key Vocabulary

commentary	impersonal	active verb
review	message	passive verb
personal	connective	

Use a performance poem as a model

Planning and Teaching

Text type	Performance poem
Literacy objective	To use performance poems as models to write and to produce poetry in polished forms through revising, redrafting and presentation.
Starwriter task	Use the poem 'Fruit Picking' as a model to write one called 'Sweet Treats'.
Suggestions for differentiation	▲ Use the poem as a model to write one called 'Sweet Treats'. When you are happy with your draft, write notes to tell a group of people how you want them to perform it.
	▼ Use 'Fruit Picking' as a model to write two stanzas of a poem called 'Sweet Treats' that begins: 'Chocolate, peppermint, toffee and creams ... '

Using the CD

Stimulus description

- An animation accompanies a reading of the poem 'Fruit Picking' by Jack Ousbey.
- Text of the poem appears on screen.
- Animated images of sweets appear on screen to inspire the children to write a poem called 'Sweet Treats'.

Using the Starwriter stimulus

- Select 'Screen Off' and play audio only. *What do you notice about the sound of the poem? How would you describe the mood? What creates these effects?*
- Return to the start of the poem. Select 'Screen On' to play the video as well as audio. *How does the animation fit the poem? How does it add to the overall presentation of the poem? What about the music and sound effects?*
- Show the poem. Encourage the children to join in with reading aloud with appropriate expression, tone and pace. *Why is it a good poem for performance? How could we perform it?* Record suggestions for sound effects, movements and actions on sticky notes around the poem.
- Discuss the structure of the poem. Ask the children to identify patterns and use the tools to highlight repeated phrases, label the number of lines in each stanza, circle rhyming words and so on.
- Show the sweet images. *Which type of sweet has the most rhyming possibilities?* Brainstorm rhyming words for different types of sweet. Use sticky notes to record the lists of possibilities on screen.
- Discuss ideas for different verses in the poem. *The fruit poem is about picking fruit. What could 'Sweet Treats' be about?* Record suggestions in thought bubbles on the screen.
- Before the children begin to write, play the audio of the poem so they keep the beat and pattern in their heads.

Using Shared Writing

The Shared Writing section uses the first verse of the poem *'Fruit Picking'* as a model for writing a new poem.

- Identify and highlight the rhyming pattern. Clap and mark up the rhythm.
- Use the hide/reveal text tool to block out 'fruit' words and replace with different sweets.
- Identify which words and phrases no longer make sense in the context of sweets and replace with alternative suggestions.

Revisiting and extending the stimulus

- Select some of the images to use in a fun health education campaign to encourage people to eat more fruit. Write the voiceover to accompany the images. Be persuasive but also explain *why* we should eat more fruit.
- Use the sweet images to write an advertisement for a new brand of sweets. Use as many persuasive techniques as you can to persuade people to buy your sweets. Read the adverts over the on-screen pictures to evaluate their effectiveness.
- Imagine that instead of a poem *'Fruit Picking'* is a story for young children. Develop ideas for the fruit characters and plot out the events. Write your story using a style appropriate for your intended audience.

📖 Writer's Guide: Support for the Task

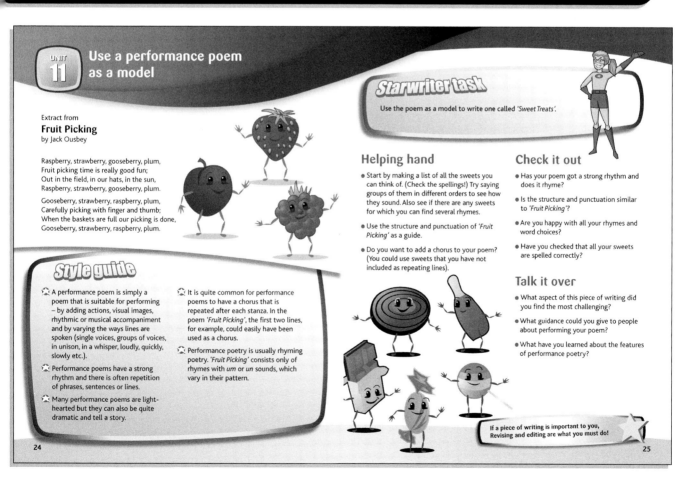

UNIT 11

Use a performance poem as a model

Starwriter task

Use the poem as a model to write one called *'Sweet Treats'*.

Extract from
Fruit Picking
by Jack Ousbey

Raspberry, strawberry, gooseberry, plum,
Fruit picking time is really good fun;
Out in the field, in our hats, in the sun,
Raspberry, strawberry, gooseberry, plum.

Gooseberry, strawberry, raspberry, plum,
Carefully picking with finger and thumb;
When the baskets are full our picking is done,
Gooseberry, strawberry, raspberry, plum.

Helping hand

- Start by making a list of all the sweets you can think of. (Check the spellings!) Try saying groups of them in different orders to see how they sound. Also see if there are any sweets for which you can find several rhymes.
- Use the structure and punctuation of *'Fruit Picking'* as a guide.
- Do you want to add a chorus to your poem? (You could use sweets that you have not included as repeating lines).

Check it out

- Has your poem got a strong rhythm and does it rhyme?
- Is the structure and punctuation similar to *'Fruit Picking'*?
- Are you happy with all your rhymes and word choices?
- Have you checked that all your sweets are spelled correctly?

Talk it over

- What aspect of this piece of writing did you find the most challenging?
- What guidance could you give to people about performing your poem?
- What have you learned about the features of performance poetry?

Style guide

- A performance poem is simply a poem that is suitable for performing – by adding actions, visual images, rhythmic or musical accompaniment and by varying the ways lines are spoken (single voices, groups of voices, in unison, in a whisper, loudly, quickly, slowly etc.).
- Performance poems have a strong rhythm and there is often repetition of phrases, sentences or lines.
- Many performance poems are light-hearted but they can also be quite dramatic and tell a story.
- It is quite common for performance poems to have a chorus that is repeated after each stanza. In the poem *'Fruit Picking'*, the first two lines, for example, could easily have been used as a chorus.
- Performance poetry is usually rhyming poetry. *'Fruit Picking'* consists only of rhymes with *um* or *un* sounds, which vary in their pattern.

If a piece of writing is important to you, Revising and editing are what you must do!

24   25

Assessing and Improving

Starwriter task	Use the poem *'Fruit Picking'* as a model to write one called *'Sweet Treats'*.
Learning intention	To write a performance poem based on the structure of a model.
Success criteria ***Writer's Guide: 'Check it Out'***	• Has your poem got a strong rhythm and does it rhyme? • Is the structure and punctuation similar to *'Fruit Picking'*? • Are you happy with your rhymes and word choices? • Have you checked that all your sweets are spelled correctly?
Review with talk partner ***Writer's Guide: 'Talk it Over'***	• What aspect of this piece of writing did you find the most challenging? • What guidance could you give to people about performing your poem? • What have you learned about the features of performance poetry?

? Children's Understanding of the Text Type

Main features

• Performance poetry is poetry written to be performed aloud.

• A performance poem lends itself to dramatisation, using movement, sound effects and choral readings.

• It is often very rhythmical and uses repetition throughout the poem.

• Certain lines or verses are often used as a chorus to be repeated several times.

• Performance poems often have a strong, recognisable structure.

• The structure, verses, rhythm and rhyme all give clues to how the poem should be read.

• The purpose of performing a poem is to communicate your interpretation of the poem to an audience.

Learning from the Writing Sample on the CD

Discuss and revise

- Read the poem aloud. *Has the rhythm and rhyme been maintained throughout the poem?* Ask the children to identify parts that work and parts that could be improved. For example:
  - delete or add a word to make a line longer or shorter to improve the rhythm
  - replace a word with one that has more or fewer syllables to improve the rhythm
  - change the order of the lines or the order of words in a line so it is easier to find a good rhyme
  - experiment with different rhyming words to fit the rhyming pattern
  - identify any lines that could be used as a chorus and repeat these after each verse.

- Ask the children to read the poem in pairs. *Does it make a good performance poem? What works well and why? What could be improved or added?* For example:
  - identify words and lines to be spoken in different tones of voice or by different voices
  - experiment with different sound effects and actions
  - add annotations to help the performer.

Grammar, spelling, punctuation and layout

- *Have the stanzas been laid out correctly?*
- *Are capital letters used for the start of each new line?*
- *Does the punctuation help reading with expression? What other forms of punctuation might help with this?*
- *Is the spelling correct?*

Key Vocabulary

performance	chorus
rhythm	verse
rhyme	image
stanza	visual effect

Write a recount

Planning and Teaching

Text type	Recount
Literacy objective	To write recounts based on subject, topic or personal experiences for (a) a close friend and (b) an unknown reader, e.g. an account of a field trip, a match, a historical event.
Starwriter task	Think of a match or an event you have attended recently. Write an e-mail to your best friend and a newspaper account of the same event.
Suggestions for differentiation	▲ Write an e-mail to your best friend, an e-mail to an elderly relation and a newspaper account of the same event. ▼ Write an e-mail to a friend about switching on town lights where you live. You can invent some details if necessary. Then write about the same thing for a school magazine.

Using the CD

Stimulus description

- Stills accompany an oral recount of the switching-on of Christmas lights.
- An e-mail and a newspaper report recounting the event appear on screen.

Using the Starwriter stimulus

- Play the stimulus without audio. *What event is this? What similar events have you been to?*
- Repeat with audio. Ask the children to listen for key information about where, when, who, why.
- Click on the Text tab to show the e-mail. Ask the children to highlight comments and details in one colour and questions in a different colour. *Why have these been added to the basic information?*
- Pause on the newspaper report. Use the pencil tool to underline information that was not in the e-mail or oral recount. *How is this report different from the e-mail?*
- In the stimulus screen, use the label tool to mark the informal features of the e-mail (e.g. greeting, questions, exclamations) and the more formal features of the newspaper report (e.g. headline, opening summary).
- Show the sequence again. Ask the children to look for another interesting detail to include in the e-mail. *Step into the scene, look around you ... What do you see, hear, smell, feel?* Use sticky notes to record details. Use thought bubbles to record thoughts and feelings.
- Return to the start and ask the children to look for an interesting angle for a newspaper report. *Zoom out and look around. What is happening? Rewind or fast-forward 20 minutes. What happened earlier or later?*
- Discuss the use of quotes in news reports. *What might a shopkeeper, young child or police officer say?* Use speech bubbles to record the children's suggestions as newspaper-style quotes.

Using Shared Writing

The Shared Writing section provides an e-mail frame in which to write a recount of an event to a friend.

- Fill in the 'To' and 'Subject' box with suggestions from the children. Write 'Dear … ' to begin the e-mail. Ask the children to suggest less formal forms of greeting and replace it.

- Choose an opening sentence from the children's suggestions. Use informal language. Delete present tense verbs and replace with the past tense. Ask for suggestions to retain the conversational tone.

Revisiting and extending the stimulus

- Use the stills as a stimulus for writing a poem about winter called *'Bright Lights, Dark Nights'*.

- Imagine that the events shown are the setting for a mystery or adventure story. Think of a crime or a surprising event that might happen during the switching on ceremony. Plot out the events that follow.

- Imagine that the stills are to be used to promote this year's 'City Lights Spectacular'. Write the accompanying text or voiceover to persuade people that this year's lights will be the best ever.

- Imagine the sequence of stills is part of a TV report describing how people prepare for Christmas in different countries. Write the part of the report describing Christmas preparations in the UK.

📖 Writer's Guide: Support for the Task

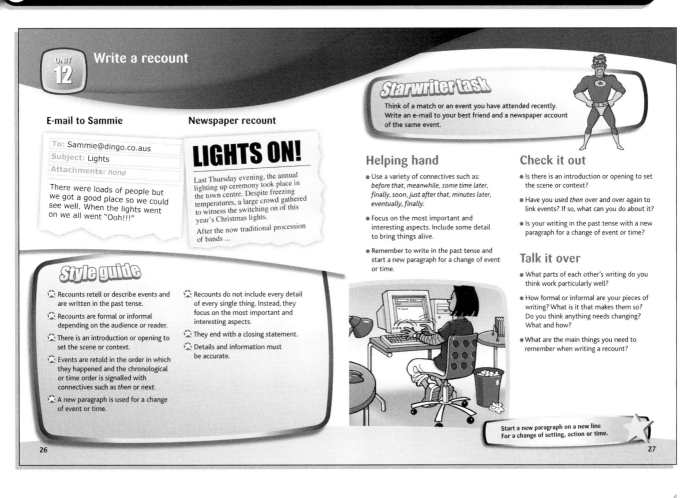

Write a recount

Assessing and Improving

Starwriter task	Think of a match or an event you have attended recently. Write an e-mail to your best friend and a newspaper account of the same event.
Learning intention	To recount the same event to two different audiences, matching style to audience.
Success criteria Writer's Guide: 'Check it Out'	• Is there is an introduction or opening to set the scene or context? • Have you used *then* over and over again to link events? If so, what can you do about it? • Is your writing in the past tense, with a new paragraph for a change of event or time?
Review with talk partner Writer's Guide: 'Talk it Over'	• What parts of each other's writing do you think work particularly well? • How formal or informal are your pieces of writing? What is it that makes them so? Do you think anything needs changing? What and how? • What are the main things you need to remember when writing a recount?

? Children's Understanding of the Text Type

Main features

• Recounts are a factual record of events that have already happened.

• They begin with an introduction to set the scene and orientate the reader.

• They end with a closing statement or comment.

• A recount is written in the past tense.

• The sentence structures and vocabulary can be formal or informal, depending upon the intended audience.

• Recounts are written in chronological order.

• Connectives are used to link events and signal the order of events.

• Important or interesting details are described.

Learning from the Writing Sample on the CD

Discuss and revise

- Ask the children to identify examples of informal writing in the e-mail and formal writing in the newspaper report. *Which words or sentences could be improved? How?* For example:
  - delete unnecessary words
  - replace weak or over-used connectives with more interesting ones
  - check the order of events is correct
  - check the language structures and vocabulary suit the intended audience
  - check the tone of the informal recount is different from the formal recount
  - delete any details that will not engage the intended audience.

Grammar, spelling, punctuation and layout

- *Are paragraphs used to signal a change of event or time?*
- *Is the past tense used for all verbs?*
- *Is the punctuation accurate and appropriate to the tone?* For example, exclamation marks do not normally feature in a formal recount but might appear in an informal recount.
- *Is the 'voice' of the recount appropriate?*
- *Is the spelling and punctuation correct?*

Key Vocabulary

formal	**connective**
informal	**detail**
past tense	**event**

Write instructions

Planning and Teaching

Text type	Instruction
Literacy objective	To write instructional texts, and test them out.
Starwriter task	Make sure you know how to send a text message. Write instructions for people who have their first mobile phone on how to text a friend.
Suggestions for differentiation	▲ Make sure you know how to send a text message. Write instructions for new mobile phone users on how to text a friend. Write instructions on what they have to do to read the reply. ▼ Work with a friend. Discuss how to send a text message and help each other to write instructions on how to do it.

Using the CD

Stimulus description

- A TV advert is shown encouraging children to teach their grandparents how to text.
- This is followed by an animation of a boy, Jay, texting instructions to his gran.
- Gran is shown receiving the text.

Using the Starwriter stimulus

- Show the stimulus. Is this a problem the children recognise? *Do you know people who can't text or don't want to learn?* Discuss the purpose and audience for the instructions.
- Show the TV images to focus on the audience. Attach thought bubbles around the images of the confused 'silver texters'. *What is confusing or worrying them? What are they thinking?* Type possible worries and confusions into the thought bubbles.
- Discuss how to make the instructions appealing to the audience (e.g. sound reassuring, make it sound simple, make it sound useful and worth doing). Type some suggestions in speech bubbles.
- Show the text instructions sent by Jay. Ask the children to use the label tool to annotate instructional features such as numbered list and imperatives.
- Ask the children to work with a partner to try them out – one reading the instruction, the other taking the role of someone trying to follow them. Encourage the 'inexperienced texter' to be particularly clueless.
- Bring the group back together. *What problems did you have? What should we remember when writing the instructions?* (e.g. give enough detail, explain *how* to do things as well as *what* to do, don't miss out any steps, explain technical words.) Use sticky notes to record these reminders on screen.
- Show an image of a mobile phone. A diagram might help in the instructions. Add labels to help identify different keys.

Using Shared Writing

The Shared Writing section shows the beginning of a set of instructions to be continued.

- Read the opening aloud. Discuss the 'You need' list. Is anything else needed?
- Annotate the instructions (e.g. numbered list, imperative verbs).
- Ask for suggestions to replace or come before item 1. Continue the instructions, checking if more information or definition of terms is needed for the intended audience, i.e. silver text phobics.

Revisiting and extending the stimulus

- Write the voiceover for another TV advert in the same series, this time with the message 'Become a silver surfer today'. Your advert should encourage more elderly people to learn to use the internet.
- Imagine that Jay's gran really gets the text bug. Write a letter from Jay to a friend about his text-mad gran. Describe how it all started when you saw an advert on TV and what has happened since.

Writer's Guide: Support for the Task

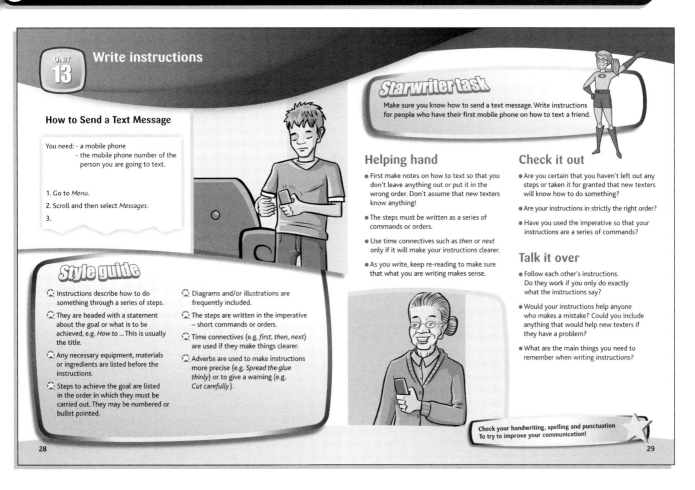

UNIT 13

Write instructions

How to Send a Text Message

You need: - a mobile phone
- the mobile phone number of the person you are going to text.

1. Go to *Menu*.
2. Scroll and then select *Messages*.
3.

Style guide

- Instructions describe how to do something through a series of steps.
- They are headed with a statement about the goal or what is to be achieved, e.g. *How to ...* This is usually the title.
- Any necessary equipment, materials or ingredients are listed before the instructions.
- Steps to achieve the goal are listed in the order in which they must be carried out. They may be numbered or bullet pointed.
- Diagrams and/or illustrations are frequently included.
- The steps are written in the imperative – short commands or orders.
- Time connectives (e.g. *first, then, next*) are used if they make things clearer.
- Adverbs are used to make instructions more precise (e.g. *Spread the glue thinly*) or to give a warning (e.g. *Cut carefully*).

Starwriter task

Make sure you know how to send a text message. Write instructions for people who have their first mobile phone on how to text a friend.

Helping hand

- First make notes on how to text so that you don't leave anything out or put it in the wrong order. Don't assume that new texters know anything!
- The steps must be written as a series of commands or orders.
- Use time connectives such as *then* or *next* only if it will make your instructions clearer.
- As you write, keep re-reading to make sure that what you are writing makes sense.

Check it out

- Are you certain that you haven't left out any steps or taken it for granted that new texters will know how to do something?
- Are your instructions in strictly the right order?
- Have you used the imperative so that your instructions are a series of commands?

Talk it over

- Follow each other's instructions. Do they work if you only do exactly what the instructions say?
- Would your instructions help anyone who makes a mistake? Could you include anything that would help new texters if they have a problem?
- What are the main things you need to remember when writing instructions?

Check your handwriting, spelling and punctuation
To try to improve your communication!

28

29

Write instructions

Assessing and Improving

Starwriter task	Make sure you know how to send a text message. Write instructions for people who have their first mobile phone on how to text a friend.
Learning intention	To write a set of clear instructions in the correct order.
Success criteria **Writer's Guide: 'Check it Out'**	• Are you certain that you haven't left out any steps or taken it for granted that new texters will know how to do something? • Are your instructions in strictly the right order? • Have you used the imperative so that your instructions are a series of commands?
Review with talk partner **Writer's Guide: 'Talk it Over'**	• Follow each other's instructions. Do they work if you only do exactly what the instructions say? • Would your instructions help anyone who makes a mistake? Could you include anything that would help new texters if they have a problem? • What are the main things you need to remember when writing instructions?

? Children's Understanding of the Text Type

Main features

- Instructions tell readers how to do or make something.
- They open with a clear heading describing what the outcome should be.
- Materials and equipment needed are listed at the beginning of the instructions.
- The steps needed to be taken are written in a logical, sequential order.
- Each step is written using an imperative verb or command.
- Time connectives are often used.
- Diagrams are often included.
- Definitions of technical terms are included.
- Factual adjectives and adverbs are used to clarify details.
- Hazards are usually highlighted as a warning.

Learning from the Writing Sample on the CD

Discuss and revise

- Ask the children to identify which sets of instructions are most accurate and easy to follow. Identify words or phrases which could be improved. For example:
  - check the instructions start with a heading describing the intended outcome
  - make sure everything necessary is included in the 'You need' section
  - add adjectives and adverbs to clarify instructions
  - experiment with re-ordering the steps to find the most logical sequence
  - add any definitions of technical terms to clarify the instructions
  - include diagrams to help readers to follow the instructions if necessary
  - add connectives to help comprehension.

Grammar, spelling, punctuation and layout

- *Have imperative verbs been used?*
- Ask the children to check for errors in spelling.
- *Have capital letters been used correctly?*
- *Are the steps listed in the correct order?*
- *Are the steps laid out in an easy-to-follow way?*

Key Vocabulary

equipment	diagram	sequence
imperative	definition	text
material	hazard	mobile phone

Make notes

Planning and Teaching

Text type	Notes
Literacy objective	To make notes for different purposes, e.g. noting key points as a record of what has been read, listing cues for a talk and to build on these notes in their own writing or speaking.
Starwriter task	Make notes on what you have seen about the Jewish faith. Use your notes to write a report about it.
Suggestions for differentiation	▲ Make notes on what you have seen about the Jewish faith. Identify any points about which you need further information. Research and make notes before writing a report. ▼ Make notes on what you have seen about the Jewish faith. Use your notes to prepare and record a talk.

Using the CD

Stimulus description

- A video of a Jewish family talking about their beliefs and how they practise their faith is shown.

- Click on the Text tab to reveal the questions asked by the interviewer (also shown within the stimulus) to provide a structure for ordering notes.

Using the Starwriter stimulus

- Show the stimulus with the introduction. At the end, ask the children what they can remember. *Could you now give a talk or write a report about the Jewish faith?*

- Rewind to one of the people from the video and pause: attach a speech bubble. Ask what the person said about a specific subject. *How accurately can you remember?*

- Click on the Text tab to show the questions the interviewer asked the Jewish family. *How could these be used to help you remember information and prepare a report?* Ask the children to 'think, pair and share' ideas for making notes and sorting information.

- Show a short section of the video. Attach a sticky note. *What are the key points?* Use the sticky note to demonstrate note making using key words and shortened forms.

- Show any image. *What does this image tell us? What key words should we record?* Use the label tool to point out important details.

- Use labels or sticky notes to provide the children with the correct spellings of unfamiliar words: Exodus, Yom Kippur, bar mitzvah, Rosh Hashana and so on.

Using Shared Writing

The Shared Writing section provides a frame for making notes prior to writing a report.

- Highlight the first bullet point. Turn the note into a full sentence.
- Discuss the difference between a note and a full sentence.
- Ask the children to suggest another note for a different heading. Delete unnecessary words and abbreviate where possible.

Revisiting and extending the stimulus

- Imagine you are going to interview a member of a different faith community about their beliefs and practices. Plan the questions you would ask to encourage them to talk about their views. (If possible, carry out your interview and write an article for your school or community magazine.)
- Write a letter to one of the people in the stimulus explaining your own beliefs and how it affects your life. Show that you are interested in their ideas and respect their beliefs.

Writer's Guide: Support for the Task

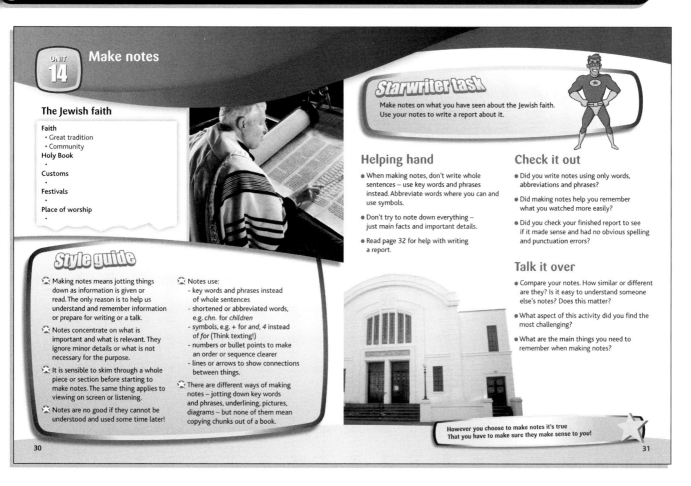

UNIT 14

Make notes

The Jewish faith

Faith
- Great tradition
- Community

Holy Book
•

Customs
•

Festivals
•

Place of worship
•

Style guide

- Making notes means jotting things down as information is given or read. The only reason is to help us understand and remember information or prepare for writing or a talk.
- Notes concentrate on what is important and what is relevant. They ignore minor details or what is not necessary for the purpose.
- It is sensible to skim through a whole piece or section before starting to make notes. The same thing applies to viewing on screen or listening.
- Notes are no good if they cannot be understood and used some time later!

- Notes use:
  - key words and phrases instead of whole sentences
  - shortened or abbreviated words, e.g. *chn.* for *children*
  - symbols, e.g. + for *and*, 4 instead of *for* (Think texting!)
  - numbers or bullet points to make an order or sequence clearer
  - lines or arrows to show connections between things.
- There are different ways of making notes – jotting down key words and phrases, underlining, pictures, diagrams – but none of them mean copying chunks out of a book.

Starwriter task

Make notes on what you have seen about the Jewish faith. Use your notes to write a report about it.

Helping hand

- When making notes, don't write whole sentences – use key words and phrases instead. Abbreviate words where you can and use symbols.
- Don't try to note down everything – just main facts and important details.
- Read page 32 for help with writing a report.

Check it out

- Did you write notes using only words, abbreviations and phrases?
- Did making notes help you remember what you watched more easily?
- Did you check your finished report to see if it made sense and had no obvious spelling and punctuation errors?

Talk it over

- Compare your notes. How similar or different are they? Is it easy to understand someone else's notes? Does this matter?
- What aspect of this activity did you find the most challenging?
- What are the main things you need to remember when making notes?

However you choose to make notes it's true
That you have to make sure they make sense to *you!*

30   31

Make notes

Assessing and Improving

Starwriter task	Make notes on what you have seen about the Jewish faith. Use your notes to write a report about it.
Learning intention	To take notes from a video clip in order to write a report.
Success criteria *Writer's Guide: 'Check it Out'*	• Did you write notes using only words, abbreviations and phrases? • Did making notes help you remember what you watched more easily? • Did you check your finished report to see if it made sense and had no obvious spelling and punctuation errors?
Review with talk partner *Writer's Guide: 'Talk it Over'*	• Compare your notes. How similar or different are they? Is it easy to understand someone else's notes? Does this matter? • What aspect of this activity did you find the most challenging? • What are the main things you need to remember when making notes?

? Children's Understanding of the Text Type

Main features

• The purpose of making notes is to help us remember information to use in another form.

• Notes help us recall key facts and information.

• Notes should be brief: key words and phrases, abbreviations and symbols are used.

• Notes should be legible and easy to understand when looked at out of context.

Reports

• Non-chronological reports describe or classify and organise information.

• Reports begin with a general opening statement about the subject.

• They are written using present tense verbs, except when they are based on historical information.

• New paragraphs are used to denote a shift of subject.

• Reports are written in a logical, not time-based, order.

• Diagrams, illustrations, captions and labels are sometimes included to help clarify information.

Learning from the Writing Sample on the CD

Discuss and revise

- Ask the children to identify examples and say why they work. *Which notes could be improved? How?* For example:
  - use key words and phrases
  - replace complete sentences with abbreviations
  - check that the meanings of abbreviations and symbols are clear and can be easily translated into complete sentences
  - note a range of connectives for future use
  - check that the notes are in a logical order.

- *How effective are these notes for their purpose? Would they help you to write a report about the Jewish faith?* For example:
  - Do they make sense?
  - Are they accurate?
  - Are they organised in a useful way?

- *How could the notes be improved to help you write the report?* For example:
  - add more key points under some headings
  - delete unimportant details
  - ensure notes are easy to understand
  - add other key words to clarify points
  - rearrange the notes in a more logical order.

Grammar, spelling, punctuation and layout

- *Is the spelling correct, including religious words and phrases?*

Key Vocabulary

abbreviation	faith
detail	belief
non-chronological	

Write a non-chronological report

Planning and Teaching

Text type	Non-chronological report
Literacy objective	To plan, compose, edit and refine short non-chronological reports.
Starwriter task	Plan and then write a report that compares the planets known as the gas giants (Jupiter, Saturn, Uranus and Neptune).
Suggestions for differentiation	▲ Plan how to organise and then write a report that compares the planets in the solar system. ▼ Use the notes you have made to help you write a short report on two or three of the planets.

Using the CD

Stimulus description

- An animated fly-through of the planets with a voiceover commentary is shown.
- Click on the Text tab to access a model section from a report comparing Earth and Mars.

Using the Starwriter stimulus

- Show the images without audio. *How are the planets the same and how are they different?* Encourage the children to use visual information, share prior knowledge and to ask questions. Record questions in thought bubbles on screen.
- Return to the start to show the video with audio. Ask the children to make notes about the planets.
- Attach a sticky note to the image of each planet and use it to record key facts in note form. Record the planet names on the screen markers to make it easy to go back and check information and compare planets.
- Link the audio and visual information. Ask the children to label features in the photos using words from the audio commentary.
- Show the text. Use the highlighter, pencil and label tools to annotate features of the report, such as general introduction, factual description, technical words and the use of the present tense.
- Read the paragraph comparing Earth and Mars. Ask the children to highlight similarities in one colour and differences in another colour. Ask them to circle the words that help to form comparisons (e.g. although, both, whereas).
- Show the image of Jupiter and then Saturn. Attach two speech bubbles to the photograph of Saturn. In one, type 'Jupiter and Saturn are the same because ... ' and in the other, type 'Jupiter and Saturn are different because ... ' Ask the children to 'think, pair and share' ideas, referring to their own notes and the notes on screen.

Using Shared Writing

The Shared Writing section re-uses the section of a report about the solar system as a model.

- Annotate the text by marking up present tense verbs, technical terms and factual descriptions. Mark up the point where the subject changes from general information to specific detail.

- Write the names of the gas giants as headings. Make brief notes under each heading of technical details to be used in the report.

- Write an opening sentence about one of the planets from the children's suggestions.

Revisiting and extending the stimulus

- Imagine the animation and photos are part of an advertising campaign for 'Solar System Tours', a company specialising in holidays in the solar system. Write the voiceover or accompanying text, persuading people that this is the perfect holiday. Try out scripts over the animation.

- Choose one of the planets to be the setting for a science fiction story. Write the opening, describing your approach to the planet and your landing. Use the notes you made previously to help you.

- Imagine you are a space traveller, speeding through the solar system. Write your space log, including interesting observations you make about the planets as they whizz by.

Writer's Guide: Support for the Task

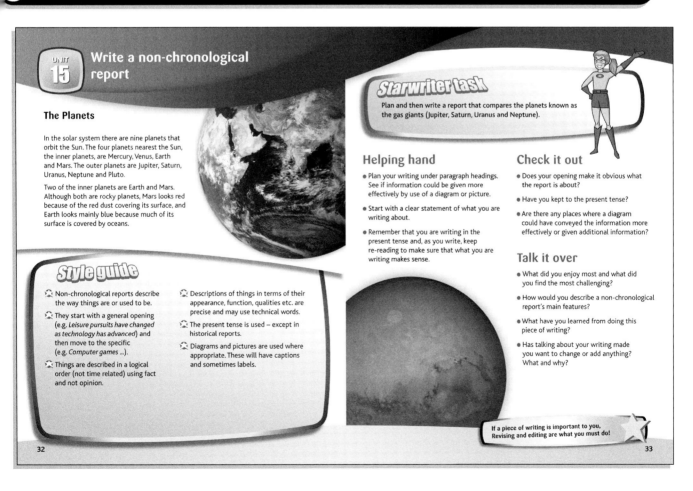

UNIT 15

Write a non-chronological report

The Planets

In the solar system there are nine planets that orbit the Sun. The four planets nearest the Sun, the inner planets, are Mercury, Venus, Earth and Mars. The outer planets are Jupiter, Saturn, Uranus, Neptune and Pluto.

Two of the inner planets are Earth and Mars. Although both are rocky planets, Mars looks red because of the red dust covering its surface, and Earth looks mainly blue because much of its surface is covered by oceans.

Style guide

- Non-chronological reports describe the way things are or used to be.
- They start with a general opening (e.g. *Leisure pursuits have changed as technology has advanced*) and then move to the specific (e.g. *Computer games ...*).
- Things are described in a logical order (not time related) using fact and not opinion.
- Descriptions of things in terms of their appearance, function, qualities etc. are precise and may use technical words.
- The present tense is used – except in historical reports.
- Diagrams and pictures are used where appropriate. These will have captions and sometimes labels.

Starwriter task

Plan and then write a report that compares the planets known as the gas giants (Jupiter, Saturn, Uranus and Neptune).

Helping hand

- Plan your writing under paragraph headings. See if information could be given more effectively by use of a diagram or picture.
- Start with a clear statement of what you are writing about.
- Remember that you are writing in the present tense and, as you write, keep re-reading to make sure that what you are writing makes sense.

Check it out

- Does your opening make it obvious what the report is about?
- Have you kept to the present tense?
- Are there any places where a diagram could have conveyed the information more effectively or given additional information?

Talk it over

- What did you enjoy most and what did you find the most challenging?
- How would you describe a non-chronological report's main features?
- What have you learned from doing this piece of writing?
- Has talking about your writing made you want to change or add anything? What and why?

If a piece of writing is important to you, Revising and editing are what you must do!

32   33

Assessing and Improving

Starwriter task	Plan and then write a report that compares the planets known as the gas giants (Jupiter, Saturn, Uranus and Neptune).
Learning intention	To write a non-chronological report using the standard features of reports.
Success criteria *Writer's Guide: 'Check it Out'*	• Does your opening statement make it clear what the report is about? • Have you kept to the present tense? • Are there any places where a diagram could have conveyed the information more effectively or given additional information?
Review with talk partner *Writer's Guide: 'Talk it Over'*	• What did you enjoy most and what did you find the most challenging? • How would you describe a non-chronological report's main features? • What have you learned from doing this piece of writing? • Has talking about your writing made you want to change or add anything? What and why?

? Children's Understanding of the Text Type

Main features

• Non-chronological reports are used to provide information about a group or class of things and describe the way these things are.

• They usually begin with a general statement about the subject.

• Non-chronological reports give information in a logical way. They are not time related.

• Headings and sub-headings are used to help the reader navigate around the report.

• They are always written in the present tense, unless they are based on historical information.

• Descriptions are factual and accurate and may include technical vocabulary and details.

• 'Compare' and 'contrast' vocabulary is often used.

• Important or interesting details are described, such as function, appearance, qualities, behaviour and uses.

• Diagrams, photos, captions and labels are used to help clarify the text.

Learning from the Writing Sample on the CD

Discuss and revise

- Ask the children to identify features of non-chronological reports and say why they work. *How could this report be improved?* For example:
  - check the opening statement clearly explains what the report is about
  - use headings, sub-headings and paragraphs to organise the information
  - make sure headings and sub-headings reflect the content of paragraphs
  - experiment with moving paragraphs around
  - include interesting facts
  - use compare and contrast vocabulary
  - use a more formal style
  - add diagrams, photos and/or captions to help clarify the text.

Grammar, spelling, punctuation and layout

- *Has a general introduction been used to begin the report?*
- Check the present tense is used consistently.
- Assess the order of the paragraphs. *Is the report easy to follow?*
- *Is the punctuation and spelling correct?*

Key Vocabulary

planet	introduction
solar system	diagram
compare	caption
contrast	

Write an explanation

Planning and Teaching

Text type	Explanation
Literacy objective	To plan, compose, edit and refine explanatory texts.
Starwriter task	Write an introductory paragraph about wind instruments and a second paragraph to explain how they work.
Suggestions for differentiation	▲ Write a piece about musical instruments. Include paragraphs to explain how simple wind instruments work and how percussion instruments work. ▼ Use the notes to help you write a short explanation of how simple wind instruments work.

Using the CD

Stimulus description

- Images and video clips of different wind instruments are shown.
- An animated explanation of how panpipes work appears on screen.
- An audio explanation of how recorders work follows, accompanied by a video clip of a child playing the recorder.
- A list of key points from the explanations appear on screen.

Using the Starwriter stimulus

- Show the opening montage. Encourage the children to suggest 'How?' and 'Why?' questions. Record questions in thought bubbles on screen.
- Show the panpipe and recorder explanations. Discuss how the information from the audio can be presented visually on screen by adding labels to the pictures, drawing arrows and writing captions on sticky notes to explain what is being shown.
- Show the bullet-pointed summary. Ask the children to use the list to check their understanding. *Use this summary to help you explain to your partner how the recorder or panpipes work.*
- Highlight the bullet point 'The air vibrates'. Use sticky notes to display 'cause and effect' connectives on the screen (e.g. so, because, this causes). Ask the children to talk with their partner and compose a sentence using the highlighted bullet point and one of the connectives. Type examples onto the relevant sticky note.
- Show one of the still images/video clips (e.g. the didgeridoo). Encourage the children to apply the points from the summary to this instrument. *Talk with your partner. Can you explain how this instrument works?* Use the bullet points and some of the 'cause and effect' connectives.
- Show images of instruments. Ask the children to choose an image to use in their explanation. *Why would this picture help your explanation? How would you use labels and captions to make the explanation clearer?*

Using Shared Writing

The Shared Writing section uses a bullet-pointed list of notes as a starting point for writing an explanation about wind instruments.

- Add any further notes to the bullet-pointed list.
- Together, decide on which of the bullet points can be used to open the explanation as a general statement. Add the list of 'cause and effect' connectives to link the points.
- Mark the bullet-pointed notes according to whether they should occur in the first or second paragraphs.

Revisiting and extending the stimulus

- Rather than writing an explanation, write a report describing different types of wind instruments. For each instrument include a description of parts and materials, its uses and details about its origin. Watch the stimulus and make notes to help write the report.
- Imagine you have to design and make your own wind instrument. Watch the stimulus to get ideas. Write a design brief to show your ideas and an action plan to show step by step how to make it.
- Use the sounds of the different instruments as the stimulus for writing a performance poem. Give your poem a repeating chorus line and make sure there are lots of opportunities to join in with making sounds.

📖 Writer's Guide: Support for the Task

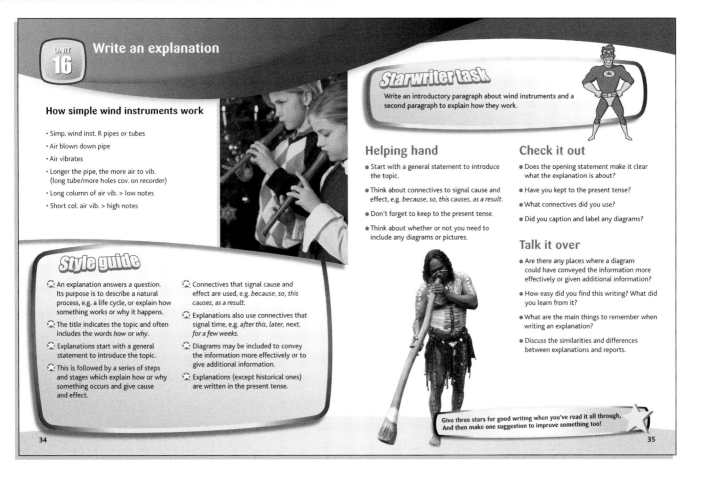

Assessing and Improving

Starwriter task	Write an introductory paragraph about wind instruments and a second paragraph to explain how they work.
Learning intention	To write an explanation that uses standard features including connectives to signal cause and effect.
Success criteria Writer's Guide: 'Check it Out'	• Does the opening statement make it clear what the explanation is about? • Have you kept to the present tense? • What connectives did you use? • Did you caption and label any diagrams?
Review with talk partner Writer's Guide: 'Talk it Over'	• Are there any places where a diagram could have conveyed the information more effectively or given additional information? • How easy did you find this writing? What did you learn from it? • What are the main things to remember when writing an explanation? • Discuss the similarities and differences between explanations and reports.

? Children's Understanding of the Text Type

Main features

- Explanations explain how something works or why something happens.
- They usually begin with a general statement about the subject.
- Explanations are written in a series of steps or events.
- They are always written in the present tense, unless they are based on historical information.
- Connectives are used to indicate cause and effect.
- Time-based connectives are used to signal a sequence of events or processes.
- Technical vocabulary is often used.
- Diagrams are sometimes used to convey information.

Learning from the Writing Sample on the CD

Discuss and revise

- Read the text aloud. *Can a listener follow and understand the information easily? How could the text be improved?* For example:
  - outline what the text is explaining in the opening paragraph
  - sequence the explanation in logical order
  - experiment with alternative examples of vocabulary that describes cause and effect
  - define technical vocabulary
  - delete unnecessary words
  - change the order of the paragraphs
  - recreate parts in a diagram instead of using text to help a reader understand the information
  - keep any diagram captions and labels brief.

Grammar, spelling, punctuation and layout

- *Has a general introduction been used to begin the explanation?*
- *Is the present tense used consistently?*
- *Is there a logical order to the paragraphs?*
- *Is the punctuation and spelling correct?*

Key Vocabulary

explanation	vibrate
cause and effect	diagram
connective	flow-chart
wind instrument	recorder

Refine and edit an explanation

Planning and Teaching

Text type	Explanation (revise and edit)
Literacy objective	To plan, compose, edit and refine explanatory texts. To evaluate their work.
Starwriter task	Choose an explanation that you have written. Discuss with a friend anything you think could be improved. Work alone to revise and edit your explanation.
Suggestions for differentiation	▲ Go through an explanation you have written and highlight anything you think could be improved. Revise and edit your explanation. ▼ Choose an explanation that you have written. Go through it with a friend and underline anything you think could be improved. Discuss how you could make changes.

Using the CD

Stimulus description

- The panpipes animation and recorder video clip from Unit 16 are shown.
- A sample of explanation text is shown on screen.
- The Starwriter character appears on screen to make changes to the text.
- A corrected version of the text is shown.

Using the Starwriter stimulus

- Show one of the images of an instrument to remind the children of the previous unit. *What did you learn about writing explanations?* Explain that in this unit they will revise and edit their explanations.
- Pause on the 'before' text and ask the children if they can suggest anything that needs improving.
- Show the complete stimulus. *What sort of changes does Starwriter make? Why does he make them?*
- Pause on the 'after' text. Ask the children to use the tools to annotate 'improvements' to language features (e.g. connectives, technical words, passive forms). *Why was the change made?*
- Rewind to show a screen image of Starwriter making a particular change. Attach a speech bubble. *What is Starwriter's point?*
- Add a thought bubble to Starwriter. Type in a prompt (e.g. 'This doesn't sound right because ... ' or 'This sounds better because ... '). Use these to prompt the children to explain the reasoning behind the change.
- Attach sticky notes to collect other useful words and phrases (e.g. other 'cause and effect' connectives or other technical verbs they might need).

Using Shared Writing

The Shared Writing section provides a badly-written explanation about wind instruments to be revised and improved.

- Read each sentence aloud and ask the children to decide how it can be improved.
- Underline sub-clauses and insert punctuation. Highlight the use of 'and'. Ask the children to suggest alternative connectives or whether to create two sentences instead of one.
- Highlight 'cause and effect' vocabulary. Ask the children to suggest how it could be improved. Delete mis-spelled words and replace them.

Revisiting and extending the stimulus

- Make an interesting and eye-catching Starwriter poster to display in the classroom giving tips for revising and editing explanations.
- Imagine that you are going to present a Starwriter demonstration showing how to improve a piece of writing. Choose a piece of your writing to use. Prepare the explanation of changes made and how they improved the finished piece of work.
- Write a Starwriter page for a school magazine. This week's feature is on 'Editing and revising explanations'.

Writer's Guide: Support for the Task

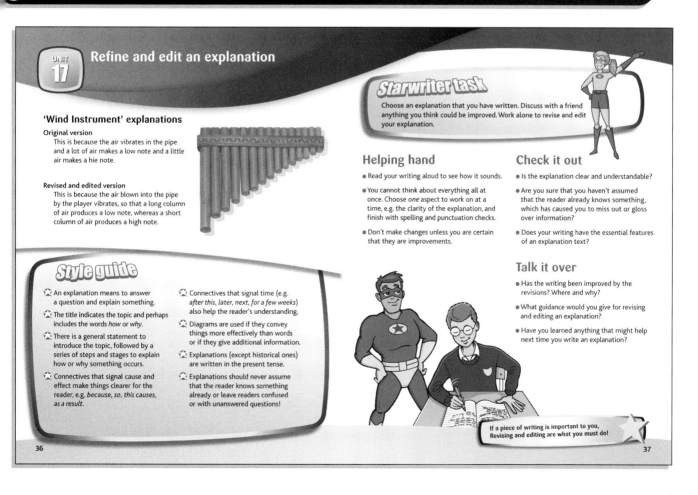

UNIT 17 — Refine and edit an explanation

'Wind Instrument' explanations

Original version
This is because the air vibrates in the pipe and a lot of air makes a low note and a little air makes a hie note.

Revised and edited version
This is because the air blown into the pipe by the player vibrates, so that a long column of air produces a low note, whereas a short column of air produces a high note.

Starwriter task
Choose an explanation that you have written. Discuss with a friend anything you think could be improved. Work alone to revise and edit your explanation.

Helping hand
- Read your writing aloud to see how it sounds.
- You cannot think about everything all at once. Choose *one* aspect to work on at a time, e.g. the clarity of the explanation, and finish with spelling and punctuation checks.
- Don't make changes unless you are certain that they are improvements.

Check it out
- Is the explanation clear and understandable?
- Are you sure that you haven't assumed that the reader already knows something, which has caused you to miss out or gloss over information?
- Does your writing have the essential features of an explanation text?

Talk it over
- Has the writing been improved by the revisions? Where and why?
- What guidance would you give for revising and editing an explanation?
- Have you learned anything that might help next time you write an explanation?

Style guide
- An explanation means to answer a question and explain something.
- The title indicates the topic and perhaps includes the words *how* or *why*.
- There is a general statement to introduce the topic, followed by a series of steps and stages to explain how or why something occurs.
- Connectives that signal cause and effect make things clearer for the reader, e.g. *because, so, this causes, as a result.*
- Connectives that signal time (e.g. *after this, later, next, for a few weeks*) also help the reader's understanding.
- Diagrams are used if they convey things more effectively than words or if they give additional information.
- Explanations (except historical ones) are written in the present tense.
- Explanations should never assume that the reader knows something already or leave readers confused or with unanswered questions!

*If a piece of writing is important to you,
Revising and editing are what you must do!*

36 | 37

Refine and edit an explanation

Assessing and Improving

Starwriter task	Choose an explanation that you have written. Discuss with a friend anything you think could be improved. Work alone to revise and edit your explanation.
Learning intention	To improve clarity and check essential features of an explanation text.
Success criteria *Writer's Guide: 'Check it Out'*	• Is the explanation clear and understandable? • Are you sure that you haven't assumed that the reader already knows something, which has caused you to miss out or gloss over information? • Does your writing have the essential features of an explanation text?
Review with talk partner *Writer's Guide: 'Talk it Over'*	• Has the writing been improved by the revisions? Where and why? • What guidance would you give for revising and editing an explanation? • Have you learned anything that might help next time you write an explanation?

? Children's Understanding of the Text Type

Main features

• Explanations explain how something works or why something happens.

• They begin with a general opening statement about the subject.

• Explanations are always written in the present tense, unless they are based on historical information.

• New paragraphs are used to denote a shift of subject.

• Explanations are written in a sequential, time-based order.

• 'Cause and effect' connectives are used to link sequences.

• Diagrams, illustrations, captions and labels can be included.

Learning from the Writing Sample on the CD

Discuss and revise

- Ask the children to identify where and how the explanation has been revised, and say why the revisions work. *How could it be further improved?* For example:
  - check the opening paragraph clearly states the subject being explained
  - check the text achieves its purpose
  - experiment with connectives
  - try using alternative causal connectives
  - include diagrams or flow-charts if necessary
  - include time-based connectives to link stages or steps
  - use new paragraphs to indicate a shift in subject or emphasis.

Grammar, spelling, punctuation and layout

- *Is the explanation introduced with a general opening statement?*
- *Are present tense verbs used?*
- *Is the explanation punctuated correctly?*
- *Is the spelling correct?*

Key Vocabulary

cause and effect   connective

paragraph   sequence

opening statement

Write a letter expressing a point of view

Planning and Teaching

Text type	Formal letter
Literacy objective	To draft and write individual, group or class letters for real purposes, e.g. put a point of view, comment on an emotive issue, protest; to edit and present to finished state.
Starwriter task	Write a draft reply to support or argue an opposing point of view. Share with a friend to revise and edit before doing a final version.
Suggestions for differentiation	▲ Write a draft letter to the newspaper expressing your views on whether technology has a positive or negative effect on our lives. Share, revise and edit the letter before writing a final version. ▼ Make a list of points you would make in reply to this letter. Discuss your list and how you might write the letter with someone. Then draft your letter. Share it with a friend to revise and edit it before doing a final version.

Using the CD

Stimulus description

- A montage of mobile phone images accompanied by ring-tone audio is shown.

- An animation of a man writing a letter to a newspaper appears on screen.

- A series of images depicting different users of mobile phones appear on screen to encourage the children to think about different points of view.

Using the Starwriter stimulus

- Play the stimulus. Ask the children to think about the different points of view represented.

- Attach thought bubbles around the image of Mr IB Wright and the various users of mobile phones. Encourage the children to suggest different opinions (e.g. 'I think mobile phones are ... because ... ').

- Click on the Text tab to show the letter. Ask the children to summarise the main points made in each paragraph and record these points below in a different colour.

- Ask the children to highlight sentences that give opinions. Encourage them to comment on these opinions

- Discuss the effectiveness of the letter. *Why is it likely to get published in the newspaper? What makes it sound impressive?* In another colour, annotate the formal language and layout features.

- Ask the children to think of points they would make in response. Discuss how to write them in a more formal way. *How would IB Wright put that?* Record suggestions in speech bubbles around the image.

- Use a sticky note to record on screen some useful phrases (e.g. 'Older people ... ', 'On the contrary ... ').

- Just before beginning to write, play the audio of the letter. Ask the children to keep the formal 'tone' or the voice of Mr IB Wright in their head as they write.

Using Shared Writing

The Shared Writing section provides a template for writing opposing points to structure a balanced argument prior to writing a letter countering one point of view.

- Fill in the points made in the letter.
- Use the highlighter tool to identify which points are fact and which are opinion.
- Fill in an opposing point to balance the argument. Ask the children to support the point with reasons.

Revisiting and extending the stimulus

- Write a story to show Mr IB Wright that mobile phones can be useful and solve problems. Use a person from the stimulus as the main character.
- Write a short character description of Mr IB Wright. Give him a name, a family and a job. *Is he a likeable man?* Decide whether to make him a sympathetic or unsympathetic character.
- Imagine that the images are part of a TV advert for a mobile phone company. The message of the campaign is: 'Everyone needs a mobile friend'. Write the accompanying voiceover to persuade people.
- You are Mr IB Wright. Write a letter to *Technology Today* magazine giving your views on e-mail.

📖 Writer's Guide: Support for the Task

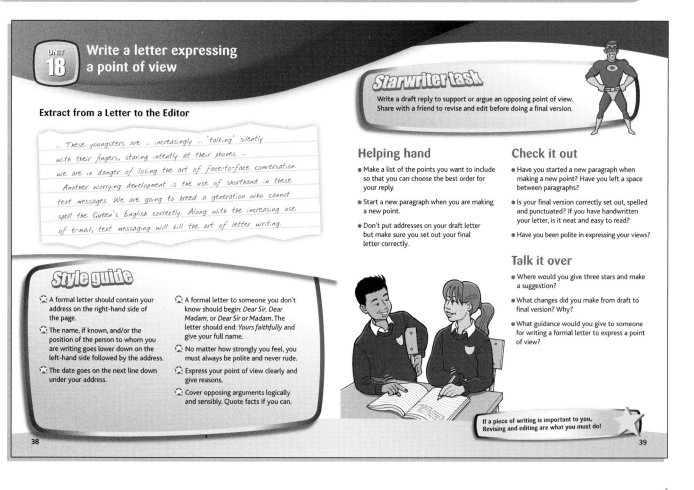

UNIT 18

Write a letter expressing a point of view

Extract from a Letter to the Editor

... These youngsters are ... increasingly ... 'talking' silently with their fingers, staring intently at their phones ... we are in danger of losing the art of face-to-face conversation. Another worrying development is the use of shorthand in these text messages. We are going to breed a generation who cannot spell the Queen's English correctly. Along with the increasing use of e-mail, text messaging will kill the art of letter writing.

Starwriter task

Write a draft reply to support or argue an opposing point of view. Share with a friend to revise and edit before doing a final version.

Helping hand

- Make a list of the points you want to include so that you can choose the best order for your reply.
- Start a new paragraph when you are making a new point.
- Don't put addresses on your draft letter but make sure you set out your final letter correctly.

Check it out

- Have you started a new paragraph when making a new point? Have you left a space between paragraphs?
- Is your final version correctly set out, spelled and punctuated? If you have handwritten your letter, is it neat and easy to read?
- Have you been polite in expressing your views?

Talk it over

- Where would you give three stars and make a suggestion?
- What changes did you make from draft to final version? Why?
- What guidance would you give to someone for writing a formal letter to express a point of view?

Style guide

- ☆ A formal letter should contain your address on the right-hand side of the page.
- ☆ The name, if known, and/or the position of the person to whom you are writing goes lower down on the left-hand side followed by the address.
- ☆ The date goes on the next line down under your address.
- ☆ A formal letter to someone you don't know should begin: *Dear Sir, Dear Madam,* or *Dear Sir or Madam.* The letter should end: *Yours faithfully* and give your full name.
- ☆ No matter how strongly you feel, you must always be polite and never rude.
- ☆ Express your point of view clearly and give reasons.
- ☆ Cover opposing arguments logically and sensibly. Quote facts if you can.

If a piece of writing is important to you, Revising and editing are what you must do!

38   39

Write a letter expressing a point of view

Assessing and Improving

Starwriter task	Write a draft reply to support or put an opposing point of view. Share with a friend to revise and edit before doing a final version.
Learning intention	To use correctly the conventions of formal letter writing.
Success criteria *Writer's Guide: 'Check it Out'*	• Have you started a new paragraph when making a new point? Have you left a space between paragraphs? • Is your final version correctly set out, spelled and punctuated? If you have handwritten your letter, is it neat and easy to read?
Review with talk partner *Writer's Guide: 'Talk it Over'*	• Where would you give three stars and make a suggestion? • What changes did you make from draft to final version? Why? • What guidance would you give to someone for writing a formal letter to express a point of view?

? Children's Understanding of the Text Type

Main features

- Formal letters are always laid out in a consistent manner, with the sender's address at the top right of the page, followed by the recipient's name and address on the left.
- If the recipient's name is unknown, the letter should begin 'Dear Sir,' or 'Dear Madam,' and end 'Yours faithfully'.
- If the recipient's name is known, the letter should begin 'Dear Mr,' or 'Dear Mrs,' and end 'Yours sincerely'.
- Formal letters written to persuade use a polite tone and standard English.
- New points are introduced in new paragraphs.
- Points are supported by reasons and factual evidence to convince the reader.
- A space should be left between each paragraph.
- Opposing points should be expressed clearly and in a logical order.
- Opinions are supported with facts where possible.

Learning from the Writing Sample on the CD

Discuss and revise

- *How successful is the content of the letter? Ask the children to identify examples of points well made and say why they are effective. Which words or phrases could be improved? How? For example:*
  - reword ideas so they are expressed more clearly
  - delete unnecessary words
  - add connectives to link ideas
  - follow up each point with a reason or explanation
  - use a variety of connectives to improve the fluency of reading.
- *Are points supported by reasons and factual evidence?*
- *Does it conclude with a recommendation? Is the conclusion logical?*

Grammar, spelling, punctuation and layout

- *Has the letter been addressed and laid out correctly?*
- *Has the letter been signed off with the correct phrase?*
- *Is the punctuation and spelling correct?*

Key Vocabulary

letter	yours faithfully
address	persuasion
recipient	in addition
yours sincerely	furthermore

Write a commentary

Planning and Teaching

Text type	Non-fiction commentary
Literacy objective	To write a commentary on an issue on paper or screen, setting out and justifying a personal view; to use structures from reading to set out and link points, e.g. numbered lists, bullet points.
Starwriter task	Make notes as you watch the film again. Use your notes to write a commentary.
Suggestions for differentiation	▲ Make notes as you watch the film again. Decide if there are areas where you need to research any facts or additional information. Make notes to incorporate these into the original ones. Use your notes to write a commentary. ▼ In pairs, make notes as you watch the film again. Use your notes to write a joint commentary.

◉ Using the CD

Stimulus description

- Images of pollution accompany a reading of the poem 'The Newcomer' by Brian Patten.

Using the Starwriter stimulus

- Select 'Screen Off' and play audio only. Encourage the children to respond to the poem. *What is the message of the poem? What pictures does it create in your head? Did you find it effective? Why?*

- Return to the start and select 'Screen On' to play the visuals as well as audio. *How do the images extend your thinking about the poem and its message?*

- Show one image. *What does it make you think about?* Add 'I think ... ' thought bubbles to record ideas.

- Show a pollution image. Put three sticky notes on the image and label them 'causes', 'effects', 'solutions'. *What has caused this? What might be the effect? Is there a solution?* Record on the sticky notes points that could be used in the commentary.

- Play the stimulus so the children can use the 'causes, effects and solutions' technique to make notes about the different sorts of pollution shown. Use labels to record key words. Record questions raised by the children in speech bubbles for further research.

- Show the 'I think ... ' thought bubbles recorded earlier. Rework these ideas into more formal statements (e.g. 'Many people believe ... ').

Using Shared Writing

The Shared Writing section uses the beginning of a model commentary as a stimulus to begin making notes.

- Use the highlighter tool to illustrate features of a commentary.
- Together, draw up a list of points as a focus for the commentary. Discuss the order in which they should be addressed.
- Together, collaborate on expanding one of the points into full sentences. Read them aloud and change to more formal, impersonal language where necessary.

Revisiting and extending the stimulus

- Use the images as a stimulus to write a collection of poems about pollution. Choose a form inspired by the subject matter, for example a 'Pollution kenning' or a shape poem entitled 'Oil spill'.
- Write a commentary on the poem that helps others appreciate and understand its message better.
- Imagine you are writing a story set in the future, where nothing has been done to stop people polluting Earth. What would the world be like? Write an opening paragraph describing the setting.
- Imagine that one of the pollution images from the stimulus is the front-page news story of your local paper. Write the news report to accompany the picture.

📖 Writer's Guide: Support for the Task

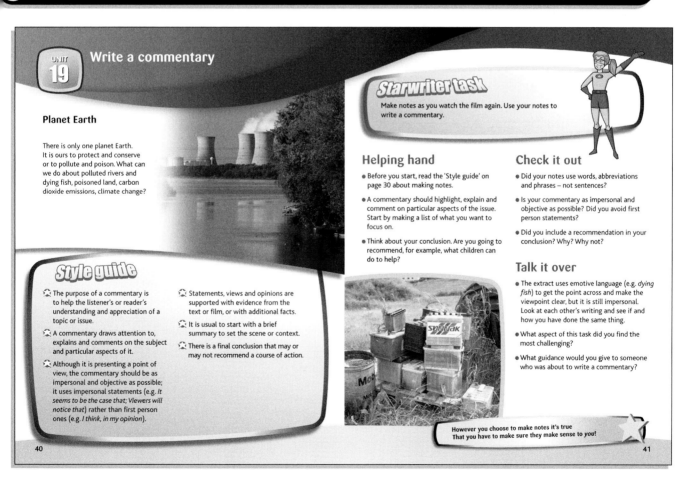

Write a commentary

Assessing and Improving

Starwriter task	Make notes as you watch the film again. Use your notes to write a commentary.
Learning intention	To write an objective commentary on the issues raised.
Success criteria **Writer's Guide: 'Check it Out'**	• Did your notes use words, abbreviations and phrases – not sentences? • Is your commentary as impersonal and objective as possible? Did you avoid first person statements? • Did you include a recommendation in your conclusion? Why? Why not?
Review with talk partner **Writer's Guide: 'Talk it Over'**	• The extract uses emotive language (e.g. dying fish) to get the point across and make the viewpoint clear, but it is still impersonal. Look at each other's writing and see if and how you have done the same thing. • What aspect of this task did you find the most challenging? • What guidance would you give to someone who was about to write a commentary?

? Children's Understanding of the Text Type

Main features

• A commentary is written to help readers understand and appreciate a topic or issue.

• A commentary does not provide the writer's personal thoughts.

• A commentary can give background information about the topic.

• Statements made in a commentary are supported with evidence.

• Commentaries often conclude with a recommendation.

Learning from the Writing Sample on the CD

Discuss and revise

- Ask the children to identify features of a commentary and say why it works. *Which words or phrases could be improved? How?* For example:
  - change active verb phrases to passive verb phrases
  - replace personal comments with impersonal language
  - use the present tense
  - use a variety of connectives to improve the fluency of reading
  - add evidence to back up points made.
- Ask the children to identify sentences, phrases or points made in the commentary that actually help their understanding of the film.
- *Are there words or phrases that explain elements of the film?*
- *Does the commentary help to explain the issues surrounding pollution? Is it clear? How could it be improved?* For example:
  - include a summary of the issues at the start of the commentary
  - experiment with reducing the number of points raised
  - delete the least important ones
  - add a reason to explain a point.
- *Does it conclude with a recommendation? Is the conclusion logical?*

Grammar, spelling, punctuation and layout

- *Has an impersonal tone and passive language been used?*
- Check the layout of the commentary. *Have paragraphs been used for introducing new points?*
- Experiment with using different connectives to link points made.
- *Is the spelling correct?*

Key Vocabulary

commentary	message	passive verb
personal	connective	conclusion
impersonal	active verb	recommendation

Construct a persuasive argument

Planning and Teaching

Text type	Argument
Literacy objective	To construct an argument in note form or full text to persuade others of a point of view and present the case to the class or a group; evaluate its effectiveness.
Starwriter task	Make notes in order to write a persuasive argument for or against: 'Should we all have the right to have fireworks?'
Suggestions for differentiation	▲ Make notes in order to write a persuasive argument agreeing with the right to have fireworks. Then write one to present the case against. ▼ Make notes in order to present one side of the argument to your group: 'Should we all have the right to have fireworks?'

Using the CD

Stimulus description

- A question is posed on screen: Should we all have the right to have fireworks?
- A sequence of a firework display is shown.
- Images and audio follows of people representing different viewpoints.
- 'For' and 'against' prompts appear on screen to encourage the children to think about their own position.

Using the Starwriter stimulus

- Show the question on the title screen. Encourage the children to share opinions. Use thought bubbles to record some of the children's comments as 'I think … ' statements.
- Show the stimulus. *What helps to convince you? Does anything alter your thinking?* Use the two prompts at the end to encourage further discussion. Use sticky notes to add points from the discussion to the two screens.
- Show some of the images of people featured in the stimulus. Ask the children to use speech bubbles to show how these people would answer the question.
- Show the list of points 'for' and 'against'. Highlight one point (e.g. 'Safe firework displays can be spectacular') Use sticky notes to display a range of connectives on the screen (e.g. if, therefore, so, because, but). Ask the children to construct a sentence using the highlighted text and one of the connectives.
- Show the public firework display again. Identify the main points made in the audio and record these on 'for' and 'against' sticky notes.
- Return to the start and show the complete stimulus again. Ask the children to work with a partner to make their own 'for' and 'against' notes. *Listen for points to use in your argument. Record points for and points against. Remember you will need to counter arguments against your views.*

Using Shared Writing

The Shared Writing section provides a template in which to organise points 'for' and 'against' fireworks.

- Together, fill in the template of points 'for' having fireworks.
- Take each point in turn and write an opposing viewpoint in the 'against' section.
- Discuss how these opposing views could be countered.

Revisiting and extending the stimulus

- Use the firework video as a stimulus for writing a poem. Choose an interesting form such as a firework- or bonfire-shaped poem, or a simile list poem.
- Write a letter or e-mail as if you were present at the display. Describe the sights, smells and sounds. Include details that will bring the event to life for your reader.
- Use the images for an advert telling young children how to enjoy fireworks safely. Write the text. Explain clearly to your audience what they should and should not do.
- Write about fireworks from an unusual point of view. For example, as if you are a frightened dog, a showy firework or an angry bonfire.

Writer's Guide: Support for the Task

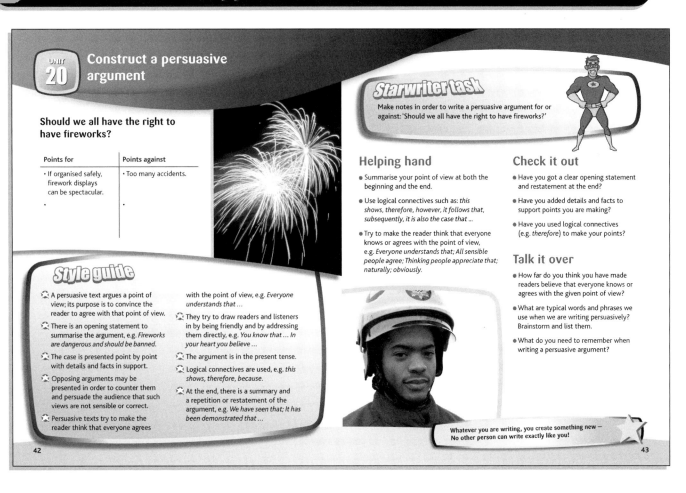

Assessing and Improving

Starwriter task	Make notes in order to write a persuasive argument for or against: 'Should we all have the right to have fireworks?'
Learning intention	To write an effective argument using the standard features of a persuasive text.
Success criteria *Writer's Guide: 'Check it Out'*	• Have you got a clear opening statement and restatement at the end? • Have you added details and facts to support points you are making? • Have you used logical connectives (e.g. therefore) to make your points?
Review with talk partner *Writer's Guide: 'Talk it Over'*	• How far do you think you have made readers believe that everyone knows or agrees with the given point of view? • What are typical words and phrases we use when we are writing persuasively? Brainstorm and list them. • What do you need to remember when writing a persuasive argument?

❓ Children's Understanding of the Text Type

Main features

• A persuasive text argues in favour of one particular point of view about an issue.

• The writer begins by stating their point of view and often gives background information about the issue.

• The writer presents a number of points in favour of their point of view in a logical sequence.

• Logical connectives are used to link points.

• Opposing points are often included and countered.

• Facts and statistics are used to support the point of view.

• Emotive language is used to convince the reader of the writer's point of view.

• A personal tone is used and readers are addressed directly (e.g. you, your).

• Persuasive text is written using present tense verbs.

• The opening statement is restated in the conclusion.

Learning from the Writing Sample on the CD

Discuss and revise

- Ask the children to discuss the notes. *Which notes could be improved? How?* For example:
  - replace complete sentences with abbreviations
  - check each 'for' point has been countered with an 'against' point
  - note a range of connectives for future use
  - rearrange the notes to provide a logical order.

- Discuss strong features of the persuasive argument. *How could it be improved?* For example:
  - include facts or statistics
  - use a personal tone and emotive language
  - address the readers directly
  - discuss and counter arguments in favour of fireworks
  - finish with a strong conclusion, reinforcing the opening statement.

Grammar, spelling, punctuation and layout

- Check the layout of the argument. *Have paragraphs been used for introducing new points?*
- *Are present tense verbs used?*
- *Is the passage punctuated correctly? Have commas been used to separate subordinate clauses?*
- *Is the spelling correct?*

Key Vocabulary

persuasion	logical	counter
argument	emotive	statement
point of view	opposition	conclusion